Essential Review

High School
MATHEMATICS II

Ira Ewen, M.S.
Principal, James Madison High School (retired)
Brooklyn, NY

Semra Kiliç-Bahi, Ph.D.
Department of Mathematics and Computer Science
Colby College
Waterville, ME

Judith Covington, Ph.D.
Louisiana State University
Shreveport, LA

Sim ter

Kaplan Books
Published by Kaplan Educational Centers and Simon & Schuster
1230 Avenue of the Americas
New York, New York 10020

For bulk sales to schools, colleges, and universities, please contact Vice President of Special Sales, Simon & Schuster Special Markets, 1633 Broadway, 8th Floor, New York, NY 10019.

Project Editors: Eileen Mager, Richard Christiano
Contributing Editors: Gregg Driben and Marti Garlett
Cover Design: Cheung Tai
Production Editor: Maude Spekes
Interior Design and Production: James Stirling
Desktop Publishing Manager: Michael Shevlin
Managing Editor: David Chipps
Executive Editor: Del Franz

Special thanks are extended to Robert Marantz and Sara Pearl.

Library of Congress Cataloging-in-Publication data is available.

Manufactured in the United States of America
Published Simultaneously in Canada

The practice tests in this book are reprinted by permission of the University of the State of New York/State Education Department.

The testing strategies in chapter 1, "Test Taking," are excerpted from *Learning Power*, by Cynthia Johnson and Drew Johnson (published by Kaplan and Simon & Schuster), and are used by permission. The information on handling stress in chapter 1 is excerpted from "The Kaplan Advantage™ Stress Management System," by Dr. Ed Newman and Bob Verini, copyright © 1996, Kaplan Educational Centers.

October 1999

10 9 8 7 6 5 4 3 2 1

ISBN 0-684-86823-7

CONTENTS

How to Use This Book vii

PART I: Study Tips

Chapter 1: Studying for Success in Mathematics 3

PART II: Diagnostic Test

Practice Test 1: Diagnostic Test 15

Answers: Practice Test 1 21

PART III: Math II Review

Chapter 2: Logic 33

Chapter 3: Mathematical Structure and Related Algebraic Skills 41

Chapter 4: Euclidean Geometry 53

Chapter 5: Analytic Geometry 77

Chapter 6: Equations and Inequalities 89

Chapter 7: Probability and Combinatorics 101

PART IV: Practice Tests and Answers

Reference Formulas for Mathematics 111

Practice Test 2 119

Answers: Practice Test 2 125

Practice Test 3 133

Answers: Practice Test 3 139

Practice Test 4 147

Answers: Practice Test 4 153

Practice Test 5 163

Answers: Practice Test 5 167

Subject Index 175

How to Use This Book

This book is designed to supplement your textbook and your class notes. As a general outline to the material you are studying, it contains the most important facts you'll need to remember to do well on your class tests, midterms, and finals. It's a powerful tool, for the student who can use it correctly. Here's how to make your test scores higher:

Study Tips

The first chapter contains some general strategies for doing well on tests. . . strategies that you may not have learned in school. Read through it and remember the valuable advice it contains.

Diagnostic Test

The first practice test is a diagnostic test—by taking it and checking your answers, you will be able to identify your weak points and begin your work of shoring them up. The answer to every question will point you to the chapter in the book where problems like the one tested in the question are further explained. Consult the relevant chapter in your texbook to further solidify your understanding of each concept.

Content Review

The chapters after the diagnostic test are a comprehensive review of the material you are learning in class. Read these in the order that will help you best. For example, if you're preparing for a final exam, you can hit the chapters you identified as weak points in the diagnostic test first, and then read all of the others later. Or, if you're studying for a weekly test, you can concentrate only on the topics that will be tested. Or, if you have some time on your hands, you can start at the beginning and read straight through to the end. There is no wrong way to read it . . . the most important thing is that you get the information you need to do well.

Practice Tests

This book contains five practice tests (the diagnostic test in the beginning of the book, and four others at the end). These are closer in difficulty to a final exam than they are to an ordinary test, but don't panic: You're the only one who will see your scores, and you have the benefit of filling the gaps in your knowledge before you're tested for real in school. If you can do well on these tests, you're well on the road to mastering this subject!

Part 1

Study Tips

Chapter 1

Studying for Success in Mathematics

You are going to do well on your mathematics tests.

You are going to do well because you will believe in yourself, because you will know the mathematics, and because you will have practiced enough of the problems so that the examination will look familiar and nonfrightening.

Think about some long-range goals, beyond the mere passing of tests, that are within your reach with some additional effort:

- You can learn the mathematics well enough to carry over the summer break and assist you in doing even better in your next course.

- You can learn the mathematics well enough to be able to apply the *concepts* and *skills* in new contexts such as science, economics, or business.

- You can learn the mathematics well enough to be able to apply what you have learned in unfamiliar settings and to problem situations in which you are not certain how to begin or where you are going. (Such situations, formally called *ill-defined problem situations*, occur continually in life. They occur at home, on the job, in school, and in your interaction with friends.)

- You can learn the mathematics well enough so that you will think of yourself as mathematically able.

Here are some of the things you can do so that the effort you put into passing your tests will reward you far beyond the day you get your passing grade.

Reflect on Your Work

After each problem you do, take a few seconds to think about the problem. What mathematical concepts were involved? Which part of the problem gave you difficulty? What question about the ideas behind the problem could you ask a teacher to help you avoid future difficulties about those ideas?

Reflection is thinking about what you have done, what you have heard, what has happened to you so that you can learn from the experience. Some people reflect on each day in their lives because they want to avoid repeating avoidable mistakes. Yet few students—or teachers—have reflected on the major concepts of their subject. What are the major concepts of mathematics? Which of these concepts applies to the current problem (or the current lesson, or the current topic)?

For your guidance, here are eleven concepts central to mathematics:

1. Sameness and equivalence
2. Evidence and certainty
3. Measure and measurement
4. Symbols and meaning
5. Characteristics and representation of data
6. Symmetry
7. Relations and functions
8. Invariance
9. Operations
10. Inference
11. Mathematical systems and models

This is not a complete list, but you might want to reflect on where other topics fit on this partial list. *Probability*? Probability is a measure (concept 3) of events; the study of probability is related closely to the study of length, area, and volume. *Statistics*? The mean, median, mode, range, and dozens of other measures (concept 3) are characteristics of *data* (concept 5). *Graphs and charts* are also representations of data.

Slope is a measure (concept 3) of a line and an *invariant* (concept 8) in a set of parallel lines.

The act of thinking about questions such as this is a powerful mode of study. It makes connections, fixes ideas in your long-term memory (the memory that lingers after tomorrow), and puts you in charge of what you are trying to learn.

Keep a Journal

A simple route to productive reflection is to keep a brief daily mathematics journal. Identify the major mathematical concepts of each day's lesson and apply those concepts to another mathematical topic or real-life situation. If you can discipline yourself to keep such a journal for two weeks, compare your grades on the material covered during those weeks to your usual grades. You will be pleasantly amazed.

Practice New Ideas by Making Up Problems and Solving Them

A rich technique for solving a verbal problem is to copy down the data and *omit the question*. Explore several things you might be able to deduce from the data given. Write one or two questions based on the data which you could answer. Often you will figure out for yourself what the question in the problem actually was!

In the days before a math test, try to make up five to ten problems that would worry you if you found them on the actual test. If you cannot solve them yourself, reflect on why you had difficulty with it. Was it unfamiliarity with the topic, with a skill related to the topic, with the underlying mathematical concept, or with the thinking skills used in analyzing the problem?

Some of the most successful students in high school and college try to predict the questions that will appear on examinations and to answer those questions. They reflect on the way the writer of the test might be thinking. Whether or not they predict the questions correctly, they are studying for the examination in an effective way. Why not try it yourself?

Thinking Skills and Problem Solving Strategies

Several strategies exist that are particularly helpful in mathematics when dealing with unfamiliar problem situations. Here are some of the most frequently applicable strategies.

Working backwards. Whenever there are several possible ways to begin and a limited objective, working backward is helpful. A good example is the proof that $\sqrt{2}$ is irrational. Because you cannot see how to begin a direct proof, you begin backward, saying, "Suppose $\sqrt{2}$ is rational." You then follow an argument that leads you to a contradiction of the theorem that every rational number can be reduced to lowest terms as a quotient of integers. Even when you know this proof very well, you would be hard put to make it into a direct proof. There are countless situations in mathematics and in life when working backward is advisable.

Finding a pattern. In mathematics, some challenging problems are easily solved if a pattern is uncovered. A teacher challenges you to count accurately the number of diagonals in a (convex) 12-sided polygon (which is known to mathematicians as a convex dodecagon). Drawing a figure and attempting to draw in all the diagonals is difficult. So try looking at simpler polygons, making a chart listing the number of sides in each polygon in the first column and the number of diagonals in the second column. With a little effort you get down to 7-sided polygons (heptagons) and your table looks like this:

number of sides	number of diagonals
3	0
4	2
5	5
6	9
7	14

You don't know *why* this pattern is developing, but you notice that the righthand column increases first by 2, then by 3, then by 4, and then by 5. Each time you increase the number of sides by 1, the number of diagonals increases by a whole number one greater than the one for the prior increase. You conjecture that the table will continue to follow that pattern:

number of sides	number of diagonals
8	20
9	27
10	35
11	44
12	54

You have made an educated guess based on limited evidence. Giving your teacher your conjecture and your evidence has a far better chance of getting you recognition than presenting a cluttered diagram with missing or miscounted diagonals.

In time you may even become skillful at explaining *why the pattern develops*. If that happens, you will be functioning much like a professional mathematician.

Adopting a different point of view. How could a strategy like this apply to mathematics? Suppose you are having difficulty understanding why the textbook has defined $x^0 = 1$, for $x \neq 0$. Instead of merely stewing about it, you decide to change your point of view and look for a pattern that might help you to understand the definition. You note that in order to get from x^4 to x^3, you divide by x. To get from x^3 to x^2, you divide by x. To get from x^2 to x^1, you divide by x, getting $x^1 = x$. You conjecture that in order to get from x^1 to x^0, you might expect to have to divide by x. Since $x \div x = 1$ (for $x \neq 0$), you can now accept the definition $x^0 = 1$ more easily.

Solving a Simpler Analogous Problem

People often do not immediately see the easiest way to do something. Solving a simpler analogous problem can lead you to a simple or complicated answer in easy steps that you will be able to construct and understand.

Let us say you are asked to determine the change in the product xy from the case when $x = y$ to the case when x is increased by 7 and y is decreased by 7. You decide to use simpler (smaller) numbers and make a chart when 1 is the increase/decrease instead of 7. You write:

Original value of x	Original value of xy	Final value of xy
1	$1 \cdot 1 = 1$	$2 \cdot 0 = 0$
2	$2 \cdot 2 = 4$	$3 \cdot 1 = 3$
3	$3 \cdot 3 = 9$	$4 \cdot 2 = 8$
4	$4 \cdot 4 = 16$	$5 \cdot 3 = 15$
5	$5 \cdot 5 = 25$	$6 \cdot 4 = 24$

In each of these five cases, the product has decreased by 1. Based on the observed pattern (strategy 2), you conjecture that when the increase/decrease is 1, the product always decreases by 1.

You now make a chart for the increase/decrease 2.

Original value of x	Original value of xy	Final value of xy
1	$1 \cdot 1 = 1$	$3 \cdot (-1) = -3$
2	$2 \cdot 2 = 4$	$4 \cdot 0 = 0$
3	$3 \cdot 3 = 9$	$5 \cdot 1 = 5$
4	$4 \cdot 4 = 16$	$6 \cdot 2 = 12$
5	$5 \cdot 5 = 25$	$7 \cdot 3 = 21$

In each of these five cases, the product has decreased by 4. Based on the observed pattern (strategy 2), you conjecture that when the increase/decrease is 2, the product always decreases by 4.

You now make charts for the increase/decrease 3, for 4, and for 5. You make another chart showing your results:

Increase/Decrease	Change in Product
1	Decreases by 1
2	Decreases by 4
3	Decreases by 9
4	Decreases by 16
5	Decreases by 25

Based on the observed pattern you conjecture that for any increase/decrease, the product will always decrease by its *square*. For the case when the increase/decrease is 7, you expect the product to decrease by 49.

Considering extreme cases. Speakers often use extreme cases to provide a useful analogy. When you use this strategy, you must be aware that the extreme cases may give insight but they may lead to incorrect conjectures. So long as you *reflect* on what you do, you can benefit from the insights and reject the incorrect conjectures.

For example, if someone tells you that a formula works for all numbers, test the formula for 0 and for 1 (the simplest cases) and for some outlandish number such as 1739. If the formula checks out in those three cases, although you have not proved it *always* works, it has a lot of believability.

Remember to *examine* the extremes, but never *depend unthinkingly* on them.

Visual representation. Sometimes a picture helps you to solve a very tricky problem.

A jogger leaves home at 6 A.M. and jogs at an irregular pace along a narrow path arriving at his destination at 7 A.M. that morning. He spends 23 hours at his destination. The next day he reverses his path and jogs at an irregular pace back home leaving for home at 6 A.M. and arriving at 7 A.M. Under what conditions must there have been a place in the road which he reached at *exactly the same time* both days?

Believe it or not, there always must be such a place somewhere along his route. If it's not obvious, draw a pair of graphs on the same axes, labeling the *x*-axis with time and the *y*-axis with distance from his home. Somewhere, the two curves in each graph cross each other. At the time and place represented in each graph—the intersection—the jogger was in exactly the same place at exactly the same time on the two days.

Intelligent guessing and testing. On a short-answer test , it is often advisable to take a shortcut to an answer by smart guessing and testing. Consider the following problem: Find three consecutive integers with product 5,814.

Setting up algebraic equations is time-consuming and difficult. You think: If the three numbers were the same, they would be the cube root of 5,814. Take out your handy calculator and compute $\sqrt[3]{5,814}$. The calculator gives you 17.98146. You guess that 18 is the middle number, and the three numbers are 17, 18, and 19. You again use your calculator to check. Sure enough, $17 \cdot 18 \cdot 19 = 5,814$.

Guessing has gotten a bad reputation because of two major difficulties: (1) teachers want students to do a problem a certain way and discourage shortcuts; (2) students tend to guess rather randomly, saying almost anything. When you make an intelligent guess, you must have a reason for your guess—it must be based on knowledge and sound intuition.

Using This Book

You will derive maximum benefit from this book by playing with the problems throughout. Reflect on them, change them, and find the central concepts they illustrate. See if you can solve each problem in more than one way, perhaps by using a different thinking strategy. When you find more than one way to do a problem, think about when you would use each approach.

Keep a "tough" file of problems that you found extremely difficult. Talk to friends and teachers about the problem and include repeated attacks on the problems in your tough file in your study plan. Nothing builds confidence as much as gaining a thorough understanding of a problem that initially stumped you.

Following the suggestions made in this section will help you to do well on your mathematics tests. And you might just find that the next math course you take will be easier and more fun than any you've taken before.

Part II

Diagnostic Test

Practice Test 1: Diagnostic Test

Part I

Answer 30 questions from this part. Each correct answer will receive 2 credits. No partial credit will be allowed. Write your answers in the spaces provided on the separate answer sheet. Where applicable, answers may be left in terms of π or in radical form.   [60]

1 The table below defines the operation $\times$ for the set $F = \{1,-1,y,-y\}$. What is the value of $(-1) \times y$?

$\times$	1	-1	y	$-y$
1	1	-1	y	$-y$
-1	-1	1	$-y$	y
y	y	$-y$	-1	1
$-y$	$-y$	y	1	-1

2 In the accompanying diagram, $\overline{OA} \perp \overline{OB}$ and $\overline{OD} \perp \overline{OC}$. If m$\angle 3 = 39$, what is m$\angle 1$?

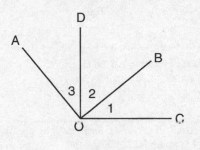

3 Solve for x: $\dfrac{x-2}{2} = \dfrac{x-1}{3}$

4 In rectangle $ABCD$, diagonal $AC = 20$ and segment $\overline{EF}$ joins the midpoints of $\overline{AB}$ and $\overline{BC}$, respectively. Find the length of $\overline{EF}$.

5 What is the total number of points equidistant from two intersecting lines and 2 centimeters from the point of intersection?

6 In $\triangle ABC$, m$\angle A = 40$ and the measure of an exterior angle at vertex B is $120°$. Which side is the longest in $\triangle ABC$?

7 What is the negative root of the equation $x^2 - x - 2 = 0$?

8 In the accompanying diagram of $\triangle ABC$, $\overline{DE} \parallel \overline{BC}$, $AD = 3$, $AB = 9$, and $AE = 5$. Find EC.

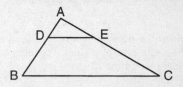

9 What is the image of $(-2,5)$ after a reflection in the x-axis?

10 In rhombus $ABCD$, $AB = 2x - 2$ and $BC = x + 8$. Find the length of $\overline{BC}$.

11 Express $\dfrac{x+2}{3} + \dfrac{x-3}{4}$ as a single fraction in simplest form.

12 In the accompanying diagram, $\overleftrightarrow{AB}$ is parallel to $\overleftrightarrow{CD}$, $\overleftrightarrow{AED}$ is a transversal, and $\overline{CE}$ is drawn. If m$\angle CED = 60$, m$\angle DAB = 2x$, and m$\angle DCE = 3x$, find x.

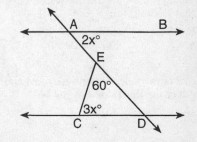

13 Find the area of a triangle whose vertices are $(-2,0)$, $(-2,6)$, and $(5,0)$.

14 If the endpoints of the diameter of a circle are (3,1) and (6,5), find the length of the diameter.

15 The coordinates of the midpoint of line segment $\overline{AB}$ are (−2,4). If the coordinates of point A are (7,10), find the coordinates of point B.

16 The sides of a triangle measure 5, 9, and 10. Find the perimeter of a similar triangle whose longest side measures 15.

Directions (17–34): For *each* question chosen, write on the separate answer sheet the *numeral* preceding the word or expression that best completes the statement or answers the question.

17 The coordinates of point (x,y) after a reflection in the origin can be represented by
(1) (x,y) (3) $(x,-y)$
(2) $(-x,y)$ (4) $(-x,-y)$

18 If the length of the hypotenuse of a right triangle is 4 and the length of one leg is 2, what is the length of the other leg?
(1) 12   (3) $\sqrt{12}$
(2) 20   (4) $\sqrt{20}$

19 Which equation represents the line whose slope is −2 and that passes through point (0,3)?
(1) $y = -2x + 3$ (3) $y = 3x - 2$
(2) $y = -2x - 3$ (4) $y = 2x + 3$

20 If the lengths of two sides of a triangle are 4 and 8, the length of the third side may *not* be
(1) 5   (3) 7
(2) 6   (4) 4

21 What is the length of an altitude of an equilateral triangle whose side measures 6?
(1) $3\sqrt{2}$ (3) 3
(2) $3\sqrt{3}$ (4) $6\sqrt{3}$

22 What is the slope of a line parallel to the line whose equation is $y = 5x + 4$?
(1) $-\frac{4}{5}$ (3) 5
(2) $-\frac{5}{4}$ (4) 4

23 What is the contrapositive of $c \rightarrow (d \vee e)$?
(1) $\sim c \rightarrow \sim(d \vee e)$ (3) $\sim(d \vee e) \rightarrow \sim c$
(2) $c \rightarrow \sim(d \vee e)$ (4) $(d \vee e) \rightarrow c$

24 What is an equation of the circle whose center is (−3,1) and whose radius is 10?
(1) $(x + 3)^2 + (y - 1)^2 = 10$
(2) $(x + 3)^2 + (y - 1)^2 = 100$
(3) $(x - 3)^2 + (y + 1)^2 = 10$
(4) $(x - 3)^2 + (y + 1)^2 = 100$

25 Given three premises: $A \rightarrow \sim C$, $\sim C \rightarrow R$, and $\sim R$. Which conclusion *must* be true?
(1) R (3) $A \wedge C$
(2) $\sim C$ (4) $\sim A$

26 In $\triangle ABC$, m$\angle A$ = 41 and m$\angle B$ = 48. What kind of triangle is $\triangle ABC$?
(1) right   (3) isosceles
(2) obtuse   (4) acute

27 If the altitude is drawn to the hypotenuse of a right triangle, then the two triangles formed are *always*
(1) congruent   (3) isosceles
(2) equal in area   (4) similar

28 The number of sides of a regular polygon whose interior angles each measure 108° is
(1) 5   (3) 7
(2) 6   (4) 4

29 Two triangles have altitudes of equal length. If the areas of these triangles have the ratio 3:4, then the bases of these triangles have the ratio
(1) 3:4   (3) $\sqrt{3} : 2$
(2) 9:16   (4) $\frac{3}{2} : 2$

30 In isosceles triangle ABC, $AC = BC = 20$, $m\angle A = 68$, and $\overline{CD}$ is the altitude to side $\overline{AB}$. What is the length of $\overline{CD}$ to the *nearest tenth*?

(1) 49.5   (3) 10.6

(2) 18.5   (4) 7.5

31 If quadrilateral $ABCD$ is a parallelogram, which statement must be true?

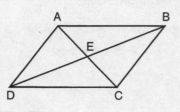

(1) $\overline{AC} \perp \overline{BD}$

(2) $\overline{AC} \cong \overline{BD}$

(3) $\overline{AC}$ bisects $\angle DAB$ and $\angle BCD$.

(4) $\overline{AC}$ and $\overline{BD}$ bisect each other.

32 How many different seven-letter arrangements can be formed from the letters in the word "GENESIS"?

(1) 210   (3) 1260

(2) 840   (4) 5040

33 What is the turning point of the graph of the function $y = x^2 - 6x + 2$?

(1) $(3,-7)$ (3) $(3,11)$

(2) $(-3,-7)$ (4) $(-3,11)$

34 A biology class has eight students. How many different lab groups may be formed that will consist of three students?

(1) 56   (3) 6,720

(2) 336   (4) 40,320

Directions (35): Leave all construction lines on the answer sheet.

35 *On the answer sheet*, construct a line through point P that is perpendicular to $\overline{AB}$.

Answers to the following questions are to be written on paper provided by the school.

Part II

Answer three questions from this part. Clearly indicate the necessary steps, including appropriate formula substitutions, diagrams, graphs, charts, etc. Calculations that may be obtained by mental arithmetic or the calculator do not need to be shown. [30]

36 *a* On graph paper, draw the graph of the equation $y = 2x^2 - 4x - 3$ for all values of x in the interval $-2 \le x \le 4$. [6]

b On the same set of axes, draw the reflection of the graph of the equation $y = 2x^2 - 4x - 3$ in the y–axis. [2]

c What is the equation of the axis of symmetry of the graph drawn in part *b*? [2]

37 Solve the following system of equations algebraically and check.

$$x^2 + y^2 + 4x = 0$$
$$y + x = 0 \qquad [8,2]$$

38 Given: $M \to N$
$\sim M \to P$
$(L \wedge N) \to R$
$\sim R$
L

Using the laws of inference, prove P. [10]

39 Answer both *a* and *b* for all values of x for which these expressions are defined.

a Solve for x to the *nearest hundredth*:

$$\frac{1}{x - 1} = \frac{x + 4}{5} \qquad [6]$$

b Simplify:

$$\frac{x^2 - 4}{x^2 + 4x + 4} \cdot \frac{x^2 + 2x}{x^2} \qquad [4]$$

40 In the accompanying diagram of rectangle $ABCD$, diagonal $\overline{AC}$ is drawn, $DE = 8$, $\overline{DE} \perp \overline{AC}$, and m$\angle DAC = 55$. Find the area of rectangle $ABCD$ to the *nearest integer*. [10]

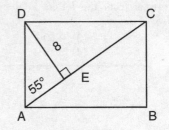

☞ GO RIGHT ON TO THE NEXT PAGE.

Answers to the following questions are to be written on paper provided by the school.

Part III

Answer one question from this part. Clearly indicate the necessary steps, including appropriate formula substitutions, diagrams, graphs, charts, etc. Calculations that may be obtained by mental arithmetic or the calculator do not need to be shown.   [10]

41 Given: parallelogram $DEBK$, $\overline{BC} \cong \overline{DA}$, and $\overline{DJ} \cong \overline{BL}$.

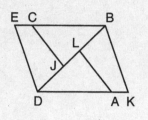

Prove: $\overline{CJ} \cong \overline{AL}$ [10]

42 Quadrilateral $ABCD$ has coordinates $A(0,-6)$, $B(5,-1)$, $C(3,3)$, and $D(-1,1)$.

Using coordinate geometry, prove that

a *at least* two consecutive sides are *not* congruent   [5]

b the diagonals, $\overline{AC}$ and $\overline{BD}$, are perpendicular   [5]

Practice Test 1

Answers

1. The correct answer is $-y$.

   Look at the intersection of the (-1) row and y column.

   You can review operations in chapter 3, "Mathematical Structure and Related Algebraic Skills."

2. The correct answer is 39.

   $m\angle 2 + m\angle 3 = 90$, so $m\angle 2 + 39 = 90$ and $m\angle 2 = 51$.
   $m\angle 1 + m\angle 2 = 90$, so $m\angle 1 + 51 = 90$ and $m\angle 1 = 39$.

   Angles are covered in chapter 4, "Euclidean Geometry."

3. The correct answer is 4.

   $\dfrac{x-2}{2} = \dfrac{x-1}{3}$ \qquad Cross multiply.

   $3(x-2) = 2(x-1)$ \qquad Distribute.

   $3x - 6 = 2x - 2$ \qquad Subtract $2x$ from both sides.

   $3x - 6 - 2x = 2x - 2 - 2x$

   $x - 6 = -2$ \qquad Add 6 to both sides.

   $x = 4$

   See chapter 4, "Euclidean Geometry" for a review of solving equations.

4. The correct answer is 10.

   $\triangle ABC$ is similar to $\triangle EBF$ so $\dfrac{AC}{EF} = \dfrac{AB}{EB}$

   Thus, $\dfrac{20}{EF} = \dfrac{2}{1}$ \qquad Cross multiply.

   $20 = 2EF$ \qquad Divide by 2.

   $10 = EF$

   Review triangles in chapter 4.

5. The correct answer is 4.

   One in each region formed by the two intersecting lines.

   You can review intersections in chapter 5.

6. The correct answer is $\overline{AB}$.

   The measure of $\angle B$ is 60° since the interior and exterior angle must add to 180°. The angles of a triangle must add to 180°, so $m\angle C = 80°$. Since $\angle C$ is the largest angle, the side opposite, AB is the longest.

   Triangles are covered in chapter 4, "Euclidean Geometry".

7. The correct answer is -1.

   $x^2 - x - 2 = 0$ Factor.

   $(x - 2)(x + 1) = 0$ Set each factor
                              equal to zero.

   $x - 2 = 0$ $x + 1 = 0$

   $x = 2$ $x = -1$

   Review equations in chapter 6, "Equations and Inequalities."

8. The correct answer is 10.

   ΔDAE is similar to ΔBAC, so $\dfrac{AD}{AB} = \dfrac{AE}{AC}$

   Thus, $\dfrac{3}{9} = \dfrac{5}{AC}$ Cross multiply.

   $3AC = 45$ Divide both sides
                      by 3.

   $AC = 15$

   $EC = AC - 5 = 15 - 5 = 10$

   For more on similar triangles, see chapter 4, "Euclidean Geometry."

9. The correct answer is $(-2, -5)$.

   A reflection in the x-axis changes the sign of the y-value.

   Reflections are covered in chapter 3, "Mathematical Structure and Related Algebraic Skills."

10. The correct answer is 18.

    The sides of a rhombus are equal.

    $2x - 2 = x + 8$ Subtract x from both
                          sides.

    $x - 2 = 8$ Add 2 to both sides

    $x = 10$

    The length of BC is $x + 8 = 10 + 8 = 18$. See chapter 4, "Euclidean Geometry" for more on the rhombus.

11. The correct answer is $\dfrac{7x - 1}{12}$.

    $\dfrac{x + 2}{3} + \dfrac{x - 3}{4}$ Rewrite with a commo denominator of 12.

    $\dfrac{4(x + 2)}{12} + \dfrac{3(x - 3)}{12} = \dfrac{4x + 8}{12} + \dfrac{3x - 9}{12} = \dfrac{7x - 1}{12}$

    Review equations in chapter 6.

12. The correct answer is 24.

    Since $\overleftrightarrow{AB}$ is parallel to $\overleftrightarrow{CD}$ and $\angle DAB$ and $\angle EDC$ are alternate interior angles, $m\angle EDC = m\angle DAB = 2x$. In ΔECD, $m\angle CED + m\angle EDC + m\angle DCE = 180$.

    $60 + 2x + 3x = 180$

    $5x + 60 = 180$ Subtract 60 from
                             both sides.

    $5x = 120$

    $x = 24$

    For more on parallel lines and transversals, see chapter 4.

13. The correct answer is 21.

    Base is distance from $(-2, 0)$ to $(5, 0)$ which is 7.

    Height is distance from $(-2, 0)$ to $(-2, 6)$ which is 6.
    Area $= \frac{1}{2}(6)(7) = 21$

    See chapter 4 for a review of triangles and chapter 5 for a review of coordinate geometry.

14. The correct answer is 5.

    Distance $=$
    $\sqrt{(6 - 3^2) + (5-1)^2} = \sqrt{3^2 + 4^2}$
    $= \sqrt{9 + 16}$
    $= \sqrt{25} = 5$

    You can review distan ces in the coordinate plane in chapter 5, "Analytic Geometry."

15. The correct answer is $(-11, -2)$.

    If coordinates of B are (x, y) then the midpoint of $\overline{AB}$ is $\left(\frac{x + 7}{2}, \frac{y + 10}{2}\right)$. Thus,

    $\frac{x + 7}{2} = -2$. So $x + 7 = -4$ and $x = -11$.

    Also $\frac{y + 10}{2} = 4$. So $y + 10 = 8$ and $y = -2$.

    Coordinate geometry is covered in chapter 5, "Analytic Geometry."

16. The correct answer is 36.

    To find middle side, $\frac{x}{9} = \frac{15}{10}$, $10x = 135$, $x = 13.5$

    To find short side, $\frac{x}{5} = \frac{15}{10}$, $10x = 75$, $x = 7.5$

    Perimeter $13.5 + 7.5 + 15 = 36$

    See chapter 4, "Euclidean Geometry," for more on triangles.

17. The correct answer is (4).

    Change the signs of both values.

    See chapter 5, "Analytic Geometry," for a review of reflections .

18. The correct answer is (3).

    Use Pythagorean Theorem, $2^2 + x^2 = 4^2$

    $4 + x^2 = 16$

    $x^2 = 12$

    $x = \sqrt{12}$

    For a review of the Pythagorean Theorem, see chapter 4, "Euclidean Geometry."

19. The correct answer is (1).

    In the form $y = mx + b$, m is the slope and b is the value when $x = 0$.

    Slope is covered in chapter 5, "Analytic Geometry."

20. The correct answer is (4).

    Because $4 + 4$ is not larger than 8.

    Review triangles in chapter 4, "Euclidean Geometry."

21. The correct answer is (2).

    The altitude bisects the opposite side, so you have a right triangle with hypotenuse 6 and one leg of 3. Thus, $3^2 + x^2 = 6^2$.

    $9 + x^2 = 36$, $x^2 = 27$, $x = \sqrt{27} = 3\sqrt{3}$

    See chapter 4, "Euclidean Geometry," for a review of right triangles.

22. The correct answer is (3).

    The slope of $y = 5x + 4$ is 5, the slope of a parallel line is the same.

    Slope is covered in chapter 3, "Mathematical Structure and Related Algebraic Skills."

23. The correct answer is (3).

    Negate both and change the order.

    Review logic in chapter 2, "Logic."

24. The correct answer is (2).

    The equation of a circle is $(x - h)^2 + (y - k)^2 = r^2$ where (h, k) is center and r is radius.

    $[x - (-3)]^2 + (y - 1)^2 = 10^2$

    $(x + 3)^2 + (y - 1)^2 = 100$

    See chapter 5, "Analytic Geometry," for a review of the equation of a circle.

25. The correct answer is (4).

    $\sim R \to C$ and $C \to \sim A$

    Logic is covered in chapter 2, "Logic."

26. The correct answer is (2).

    $m\angle A + m\angle B + m\angle C = 180$

    $41 + 48 + m\angle C = 180$

    $89 + m\angle C = 180$

    $m\angle C = 91$, so C is an obtuse angle. The triangle is obtuse.

    See chapter 4 for a review of triangles, "Euclidean Geometry."

27. The correct answer is (4).

    Similar because the angles of one are congruent to the corresponding angles of another.

    Similarity and congruence are covered in chapter 4, "Euclidean Geometry."

28. The correct answer is (1).

    The measure of each angle of a regular polygon is

    $$\frac{180(n - 2)}{n} = 108$$

    $180(n - 2) = 108n$

    $180n - 360 = 108n$ Subtract $180n$ from both sides.

    $-360 = -72n$ Divide both sides by -72.

    $5 = n$

To review the angles of a polygon, see chapter 4, "Euclidean Geometry."

29. The correct answer is (1).

    Because area is $\frac{1}{2} \cdot$ base $\cdot$ height.

    Area of a triangle is covered in chapter 4, "Euclidean Geometry."

30. The correct answer is (2).

    ΔACD is a right triangle, so

    $$\sin A = \frac{\text{opp}}{\text{hyp}} = \frac{CD}{AC}$$

    $$\sin 68 = \frac{CD}{20}$$

    $$20 \sin 68 = CD$$

    $$18.54 = CD$$

    For a review of right triangle trigonometry, see chapter 4, "Euclidean Geometry."

31. The correct answer is (4).

    Because the diagonals of a parallelogram bisect each other.

    Parallelograms are covered in chapter 4, "Euclidean Geometry."

32. The correct answer is (3).

    $$\frac{_7P_7}{_2P_2 \, _2P_2}$$

    The $_7P_7$ comes from the fact that there are 7 letters and we are choosing 7 letters. The two $_2P_2$ come from the fact that there are 2 E's and 2 S's.

    See chapter 7 for a review of permutations.

33. The correct answer is (1).

    $$y = x^2 - 6x + 2$$

    $$y = (x^2 - 6x + 9) - 9 + 2 \quad \text{Add and subtract}$$
    $$\left(\frac{6}{2}\right)^2 = 9.$$

    $$y = (x - 3)^2 - 7$$

    The value that makes $x - 3 = 0$ is the x-value of the turning point, -7 is the y-value of the turning point.

    Parabolas are covered in chapter 5, "Analytic Geometry."

34. The correct answer is (1).

    $$_8C_3 = \frac{8!}{5!3!} = \frac{8 \cdot 7 \cdot \cancel{6} \cdot \cancel{5!}}{\cancel{8} \cdot \cancel{2} \cdot 1 \cdot \cancel{5!}} = 56$$

    Permutations are covered in chapter 7, "Probability and Combinatorics."

35.

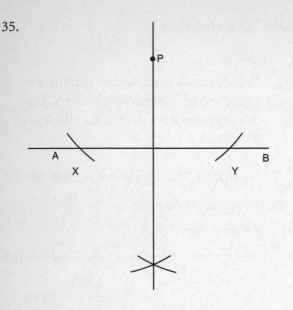

1. Extend *AB* on one or both sides if necessary.

2. Swing an arc from *P* to *AB*. Mark intersection, *X* and *Y*.

3. Bisect $\overline{XY}$ by swinging same size arcs from *X* and *Y*.

4. Connect arc intersections.

For more information on this topic, consult the relevant chapter in your textbook.

36.

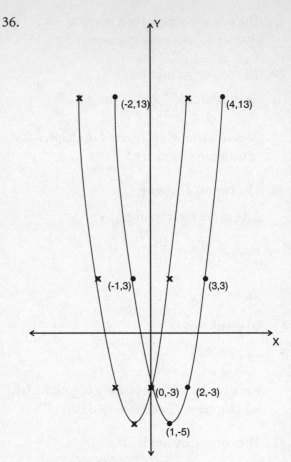

a. on graph paper.

b. on graph paper. Change the sign of the *x*-values.

c. $x = -1$

The vertical line through the turning point.

You can review parabolas in chapter 5.

37. $(0, 0)$ and $(-2, 2)$

Solve $y + x = 0$ for x to get $x = -y$

Substitute into $x^2 + y^2 + 4x = 0$ to get

$(-y)^2 + y^2 - 4y = 0$

$y^2 + y^2 - 4y = 0$

$2y^2 - 4y = 0$ Factor

$2y(y - 2) = 0$ Set each factor equal to 0

$2y = 0$ $y - 2 = 0$

$y = 0$ $y = 2$

$x = -y = 0$ $x = -y = -2$

Check $(0, 0)$ $0 + 0 = 0$ √

$(0)^2 + (0)^2 + 4(0) = 0$ √

Check $(-2, 2)$ $2 + (-2) = 0$ √

$(-2)^2 + (2)^2 + 4(-2) = 0$

$4 + 4 - 8 = 0$ √

For further review of solving a system of equations, see chapter 6.

38.

Statements of direct proof	Reasons
1. $(L \wedge N) \rightarrow R$	Given
2. $\sim R \rightarrow \sim(L \wedge N)$	Law of contrapositive applied to step 1.
3. $\sim R$	Given
4. $\sim(L \wedge N)$	Law of detachment applied to steps 2 and 3.
5. $\sim L \vee \sim N$	De Morgan's law applied to step 4.
6. L	Given
7. $\sim N$	Law of disjunctive inference applied to steps 5 and 6
8. $M \rightarrow N$	Given
9. $\sim N \rightarrow \sim M$	Law of contrapositive applied to step 8
10. $\sim M$	Law of detachment applied to steps 7 and 9
11. $\sim M \rightarrow P$	Given
12. P	Law of detachment applied to steps 11 and 13.

See chapter 2 for a review of logic.

39. a.   1.85 and -4.85

$$\frac{1}{x-1} = \frac{x+4}{5} \qquad \text{Cross multiply.}$$

$$5 = (x-1)(x+4)$$

$$5 = x^2 + 4x - x - 4$$

$$0 = x^2 + 3x - 9$$

$$x = \frac{-3 \pm \sqrt{9 - 4(1)(-9)}}{2(1)}$$

$$= \frac{-3 \pm \sqrt{9 + 36}}{2}$$

$$= \frac{-3 \pm \sqrt{45}}{2}$$

$$\frac{-3 + \sqrt{45}}{2} = 1.85 \qquad \frac{-3 - \sqrt{45}}{2} = -4.85$$

b. $\dfrac{x-2}{x}$

$$\frac{x^2 - 4}{x^2 + 4x + 4} \cdot \frac{x^2 + 2x}{x^2}$$

Factor then cancel common factors between numerator and denominator.

$$\frac{\cancel{(x+2)}(x-2)}{\cancel{(x+2)}(x+2)} \cdot \frac{x\cancel{(x+2)}}{x^2} = \frac{x-2}{x}$$

You can review the quadratic formula in chapter 6.

40. The correct answer is 136.

In $\triangle DAE$, $\sin 55 = \dfrac{\text{opp}}{\text{hyp}} = \dfrac{DE}{AD} = \dfrac{8}{AD}$

$$\sin 55 = \frac{8}{AD}$$

$$AD \sin 55 = 8$$

$$AD = \frac{8}{\sin 55} = 9.77$$

In $\triangle DAC$, $\tan 55 = \dfrac{\text{opp}}{\text{adj}} = \dfrac{DC}{AD} = \dfrac{DC}{9.77}$

$$\tan 55 = \frac{DC}{9.77}$$

$$9.77 \tan 55 = DC$$

$$13.95 = DC$$

$$\text{Area} = (AD)(DC) = (9.77)(13.95) = 136.29$$

Right triangle trigonometry is covered in chapter 4.

41. It is given that $\overline{BC} \cong \overline{DA}$. Since $\overline{BE} \parallel \overline{DK}$ and $\angle EBD$ and $\angle BDK$ are alternate interior angles, $\angle EBD \cong \angle BDK$. Since $\overline{DJ} \cong \overline{BL}$, $DJ + JL = BL + JL$, so $DL = BJ$, that is $\overline{DL} \cong \overline{BJ}$. Thus $\triangle BCJ \cong \triangle DAL$ by SAS. Since $\overline{CJ}$ and $\overline{AL}$ are corresponding parts of congruent triangles, $\overline{CJ} \cong \overline{AL}$

For a review of geometric proofs, see chapter 4.

42.

a. $AB =$

$\sqrt{(5-0)^2 + [-1-(-6)]^2} = \sqrt{5^2 + 5^2} =$

$\sqrt{25 + 25} = \sqrt{50}$

$BC =$

$\sqrt{(3-5)^2 + [3-(-1)]^2} =$
$\sqrt{(-2)^2 + (-4)^2} =$

$\sqrt{4 + 16} = \sqrt{20}$

So $AB \neq BC$.

Note that $\overline{AB}$ and $\overline{BC}$ are not congruent.

b. The slope of $\overline{AC}$ is $\dfrac{3-(-6)}{3-0} = \dfrac{9}{3} = 3$

The slope of $\overline{BD}$ is

$\dfrac{1-(-1)}{-1-5} = \dfrac{2}{-6} = -\dfrac{1}{3}$

The slopes are negative reciprocals so the lines are perpendicular.

See chapter 5 for a review of coordinate geometry.

Part III

Math II Review

Chapter 2

Logic

A. Review of Logic from Math I

1. Logical connectives and truth value

A *statement* is a sentence that has a truth value, that is, the sentence is either true or false.

Let's consider the truth values for combinations of statements.

The *conjunction* $p \wedge q$ of two statements p and q is true if p and q are both true, and is false otherwise.

The *disjunction* $p \vee q$ of two statements p and q is false if p and q are both false, and is true otherwise.

The *negation* $(\sim p)$ of a statement is a statement whose truth value is always opposite of the original statement.

A *conditional statement* $(p \rightarrow q)$ is a statement that can be put in the form "if p, then q." It is false if p is true and q is false, and it is true otherwise. The statement p is called the *hypothesis* or *antecedent* of the conditional and q is called the *conclusion* or *consequent*.

A *biconditional statement* $p \leftrightarrow q$ is defined to be $(p \rightarrow q) \wedge (q \rightarrow p)$.

A statement that is always true, regardless of the truth values of its component parts, is called a *tautology*. A statement that is always false is called a *contradiction*.

The truth values for the combined statements are summarized in the following table:

p	q	$p \wedge q$	$p \vee q$	$p \rightarrow q$	$p \leftrightarrow q$
T	T	T	T	T	T
T	F	F	T	F	F
F	T	F	T	T	F
F	F	F	F	T	T

33

Example 1:

Decide which one of the following sentences is a statement:

p: Julius Caesar is dead.

q: $1 + 1 = 5$

r: Pythagoras had an egg for his breakfast on his tenth birthday.

Solution:

Among the three sentences, *p* is a true statement and *q* is a false statement. Since we can never know whether the sentence *r* is true or false, it is not a statement.

Example 2:

If *p:* The numbers 2 and 3 are prime numbers, and *q:* Every triangle is isosceles, find the truth values of $p \wedge q$, and $p \vee q$.

Solution:

Since *p* is true and *q* is false, $p \wedge q$ is false, and $p \vee q$ is true.

2. Related conditionals

   a. The *converse* of a conditional statement $p \rightarrow q$ is the statement $q \rightarrow p$, formed by interchanging the hypothesis and the conclusion.

   b. The *inverse of* $p \rightarrow q$ is the statement $(\sim p) \rightarrow (\sim q)$, formed by negating both the hypothesis and the conclusion.

   c. The *contrapositive* of $p \rightarrow q$ is the statement $(\sim q) \rightarrow (\sim p)$, formed by negating and interchanging the roles of the hypothesis and the conclusion.

   We can summarize these definitions as follows:

A conditional	If *p*, then *q*	$p \rightarrow q$
Its converse	If *q*, then *p*	$q \rightarrow p$
Its inverse	If not *p*, then not *q*	$(\sim p) \rightarrow (\sim q)$
Its contrapositive	If not *q*, then not *p*	$(\sim q) \rightarrow (\sim p)$

Example 1:

Conditional: "If two sides of a triangle have equal length, then the triangle is an isosceles triangle."

Converse: "If a triangle is an isosceles triangle, then two of its sides have equal length."

Inverse: "If two sides of a triangle do not have equal length, then the triangle is not an isosceles triangle."

Contrapositive: "If a triangle is not an isosceles triangle, then two sides of the triangle do not have equal length."

B. Laws of Reasoning

1. *Law of Detachment* states that if a conditional statement and its hypothesis are true, then its conclusion is true.

   Example 1:

   Suppose that the statement, "If David wins, Mike loses" is true. Further, suppose David won. Conclusion: Mike lost.

2. *Law of Contrapositive* states that a conditional statement $p{\rightarrow}q$ and its contrapositive $({\sim}q){\rightarrow}({\sim}p)$ have the same truth value. One can observe this fact by constructing the truth value of $p{\rightarrow}q$ and $({\sim}q){\rightarrow}({\sim}p)$ as follows:

p	q	$\sim q$	$\sim p$	$p{\rightarrow}q$	$({\sim}q){\rightarrow}({\sim}p)$
T	T	F	F	T	T
T	F	T	F	F	F
F	T	F	T	T	T
F	F	T	T	T	T

   Example 1:

   Conditional: If $a = 2$, then $a + 3 = 5$.

   Contrapositive: If $a + 3 \neq 5$, then $a \neq 2$.

3. *Law of Disjunctive Inference* states that if a disjunction $(p{\vee}q)$ is true and one of its component parts is false, then the other component must be true. We can observe that the condition of the law is satisfied in the two framed cases, and in both cases the conclusion of the law holds.

p	q	$p{\vee}q$
T	T	T
T	F	T
F	T	T
F	F	F

Example 1:

Let p: Emily wins, q: Daren wins. Suppose $p \lor q$: Emily wins or Daren wins is a true statement. Daren does not win. Conclusion: Emily wins.

Example 2:

Let p: The number x is negative, q: the number y is negative. Then $p \lor q$: The number x or the number y is negative. Suppose $p \lor q$ is a true statement. Further, suppose the number x is positive, that is, p is false. Conclusion: The number y is negative.

4. *Law of Syllogism* combines two conditional $p \to q$ and $q \to r$ to produce a third conditional $p \to r$, as follows: $[(p \to q) \land (q \to r)] \leftrightarrow (p \to r)$.

Example 1:

Let p: I am happy, q: I sing, r: My brother is not happy.

$p \to q$: If I am happy, I sing. $q \to r$: If I sing, my brother is not happy. $p \to r$: If I am happy, my brother is not happy.

Example 2:

Let p: $5x + 1 = 21$, q: $5x = 20$, r: $x = 4$. Then if $5x + 1 = 21$, $5x = 21$. If $5x = 20$, then $x = 4$. Hence, if $5x + 1 = 20$, $x = 4$.

5. *De Morgan's laws* establish the effect of negation on the conjunction and disjunction of two statements p and q.

Law 1. $\sim (p \land q) \leftrightarrow (\sim p) \lor (\sim q)$

Law 2. $\sim (p \lor q) \leftrightarrow (\sim p) \land (\sim q)$

Example 1:

Use De Morgan's laws to rewrite the following statement as a combination of two simpler, negative statements.

"It is not true that I went to the movies and ate too much popcorn."

Let p: I went to the movies, and q: I ate too much popcorn. Then the statement is $\sim (p \land q)$, which is equivalent to $(\sim p) \lor (\sim q)$ by De Morgan's law 1. Since $(\sim p)$: I did not go to the movies, and $(\sim q)$: I did not eat too much popcorn, $(\sim p) \lor (\sim q)$: I did not go to the movies or I did not eat too much popcorn.

C. Development of Notions of Proof

   1. Direct Proof

To prove a statement true, we construct an argument starting with a hypothesis that is known to be true and ending with the statement in question. This type of argument is called a *direct proof* of the statement.

Example 1:

Four balls labeled as A, B, C, and D are put in a box. Determine the red colored ball if you are given the following information:

Either A or B is red. If B is red, then C is green. If C is green, then D is not blue. We know that D is blue.

Solution:

Let p: A is red, q: B is red, r: C is green, and s: D is blue. Then we are given:

$p \lor q$: Either A or B is red.

$q \to r$: If B is red, then C is green.

$r \to (\sim s)$: If C is green, then D is not blue.

s: D is blue

Steps of direct proof	Reasons
1. $q \to r$	Given
2. $r \to (\sim s)$	Given
3. $q \to (\sim s)$	Law of syllogism applied to steps 1 and 2
4. s	Given
5. $s \to (\sim q)$	Law of contrapositive applied to step 3
6. $\sim q$	Law of detachment applied to steps 4 and 5
7. $p \lor q$	Given
8. p	Law of disjunctive inference applied to 6 and 7

Therefore, p is true, that is, A is red.

2. Indirect Proof

We may prove the truth of a statement p by forming its negation, $\sim p$, and using $\sim p$ as the hypothesis of a valid argument whose conclusion is known to be false. This implies that $\sim p$ must itself be false, and hence p must be true. This procedure is called *indirect proof*.

Example 1:

Using the example from the previous section, let's prove *indirectly* that the ball A is red.

Steps of indirect proof	Reasons
1. $\sim p$	Assumption
2. $p \vee q$	Given
3. q	Law of disjunctive inference applied to steps 1 and 2
4. $q \rightarrow r$	Given
5. r	Law of detachment applied to steps 3 and 4
6. $r \rightarrow (\sim s)$	Given
7. $\sim s$	Law of detachment applied to steps 5 and 6
8. s	Given
9. $(\sim s) \wedge s$ is always false; that is, we have a contradiction.	Definition of conjunction (also see question 1)
10. $\sim(\sim p)$	If an assumption leads to a contradiction, it must be false
11. p	Law of double negative

Questions

1. Show that regardless of the truth value of p, $p \vee (\sim p)$ is always true and $p \wedge (\sim p)$ is always false.

2. If p: All animals have fur, and q: The area of a circle of radius 1 is π, which of the following are true and which are false?

   a. $\sim p$
   b. $\sim q$
   c. $(\sim p) \wedge q$
   d. $p \vee (\sim q)$
   e. $p \rightarrow q$
   f. $q \rightarrow p$
   g. $(\sim p) \rightarrow (\sim q)$
   h. $(\sim q) \rightarrow (\sim p)$

In Exercises 3–6, write the given statements in symbolic form using p and q to represent simple, positive statements.

3. If Jim plays, then the team wins.

4. That tree is either an oak or a maple.

5. It is false that the state governor is either a Democrat or a Republican.

6. I like mathematics and chemistry.

7. Use truth tables to prove

   a. $p \vee \sim (p \wedge q)$ is a tautology.
   b. $\sim (p \wedge (\sim q)) \leftrightarrow (\sim p) \vee q$ is a tautology.

Answers

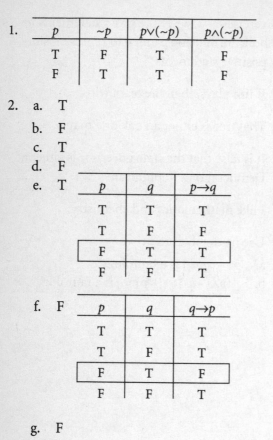

1.

p	~p	p∨(~p)	p∧(~p)
T	F	T	F
F	T	T	F

2. a. T
   b. F
   c. T
   d. F
   e. T

p	q	p→q
T	T	T
T	F	F
F	T	T
F	F	T

   f. F

p	q	q→p
T	T	T
T	F	T
F	T	F
F	F	T

   g. F

p	q	~p	~q	~p→~q
T	T	F	F	T
T	F	F	T	T
F	T	T	F	F
F	F	T	T	T

   h. T

p	q	~p	~q	~q→~p
T	T	F	F	T
T	F	F	T	F
F	T	T	F	T
F	F	T	T	T

3. If p: Jim plays, and q: The team wins, p→q: If Jim plays, the team wins.

4. If p: That tree is oak, and q: That tree is maple, p∨q: That tree is either an oak or a maple.

5. If p: The state governor is a Democrat, and q: The state governor is a Republican, ~(p∨q): It is false that the state governor is either a Democrat or a Republican.

6. If p: I like mathematics, and q: I like chemistry, p∧q: I like mathematics and chemistry.

7. a.

p	q	p∧q	~(p∧q)	p∨~(p∧q)
T	T	T	F	T
T	F	F	T	T
F	T	F	T	T
F	F	F	T	T

   b.

p	q	p∧(~q)	~[p∧(~q)]	(~p)∨q	~[p∧(~q)]↔[(~p)∨q]
T	T	F	T	T	T
T	F	T	F	F	T
F	T	F	T	T	T
F	F	F	T	T	T

Chapter 3

Mathematical Structure and Related Algebraic Skills

A. Review of Properties of the Real Numbers

An operation *, on a set S, is any rule or process that assigns to each ordered pair of elements of S exactly one element of that set S.

1. Closure

    The set S is closed under the operation * if $a * b$ is in S, for all a and b in S. This property is called closure.

2. Commutative

    An operation *, on a set S, is commutative if $a * b = b * a$ for all elements a and b in S.

3. Associative

    An operation, *, on a set S, is associative if $(a * b) * c = a * (b * c)$ for all elements a, b, and c in S.

4. Identity element

    The element, e, is an identity element if for all a in S, $a * e = e * a = a$.

5. Inverse element

    For a and b in S, if $a * b = b * a = e$, b is called the inverse of a.
    For example, in the real numbers, if the operation is $\oplus$, -5 is the inverse of 5, since $5 + (-5) = 0$.

Example 1:

The following table defines an operation, *, on the set $S = \{a, b, c, d\}$. The first column represents the first component, and the first row represents the second component of the operation *. For example, $a * c = b$, $b * d = d$, and $d * c = a$.

Find

a. the identity element

b. the inverse of a

and decide

c. if * is commutative

*	a	b	c	d
a	c	a	b	b
b	a	b	c	d
c	b	c	a	d
d	d	d	a	c

Solution:

a. Since $a * b = b * a = a$, $b * b = b$, $c * b = b * c = c$, and $d * b = b * d = d$, b is the identity element.

b. Since $a * c = c * a = b$, c is the inverse of a.

c. It is not commutative. Observe that

$c * d = d$ and $d * c = a$;

6. Distributive Property

Let $\oplus$ and $\otimes$ be two operations on S. The operation $\otimes$ is said to distribute over $\oplus$ if $a \otimes (b \oplus c) = (a \otimes b) \oplus (a \otimes c)$, for all a, b, and c in S.

7. The importance of the Properties of the Real Numbers:

They give us the necessary tools to add and multiply polynomials.

B. Review of Algebraic Skills

1. Addition of polynomials

Addition of polynomials is achieved by combining the like terms of the polynomials being added and writing the result in simplest form.

Example 1:

Let $p(x) = 2x^2 - 3x$ and $q(x) = 5x + 7$. Then

$$
\begin{aligned}
p(x) + q(x) &= (2x^2 - 3x) + (5x + 7) \\
&= 2x^2 - 3x + 5x + 7 \\
&= 2x^2 + (-3x + 5x) + 7 \\
&= 2x^2 + 2x + 7
\end{aligned}
$$

2. Multiplication of polynomials

We rely heavily on the distributive property when multiplying polynomials.

Example 1:

Let $p(x) = 3x^2$ and $q(x) = x^2 + 4x - 3$. Then

$$
\begin{aligned}
p(x)\, q(x) &= 3x^2 (x^2 + 4x - 3) \\
&= 3x^2(x^2) + 3x^2(4x) + 3x^2(-3) \quad \text{by the distributive property} \\
&= 3x^4 + 12x^3 - 9x^2 \quad \text{by the laws of exponents}
\end{aligned}
$$

Example 2:

Let $p(x) = (x - 3)$ and $q(x) = (2x + 1)$. Then

$$p(x)\, q(x) \quad = (x - 3)\,(2x + 1)$$

$$= (x - 3)(2x) + (x - 3)(1) \qquad \text{by the distributive property}$$

$$= x(2x) + (-3)(2x) + x(1) + (-3)(1) \quad \text{by the distributive property}$$

$$= 2x^2 - 6x + x - 3$$

$$= 2x^2 - 5x - 3 \qquad \text{combining like terms}$$

3. **Simplification of algebraic expressions**

   It may be necessary to remove the parentheses before combining like terms.

   Example 1:

   Simplify: $5x^2 - (9x^2 - 7)$

   Solution:

   $5x^2 - (9x^2 - 7) = 5x^2 - 9x^2 + 7 = -4x^2 + 7$

4. **Division of polynomials by monomials**

   First, let's recall that if $a \neq 0$, $\dfrac{a}{a} = 1$.

   Example 1:

   Divide: $\dfrac{8\,x^3 y^2}{4xy}$

   Solution 1:

   $\dfrac{8x^3 y^2}{4xy} = \dfrac{4xy(2x^2 y)}{4xy} = 2x^2 y$, if x and y are not equal to zero.

Solution 2:

(By using the laws of exponents)

$$\frac{8x^3y^2}{4xy} = \frac{2^3x^3y^2}{2^2xy} = 2^{3-2}\,x^{3-1}\,y^{2-1} = 2\,x^2\,y$$

Example 2:

Divide: $\dfrac{20x^2y + 6xy^3 - 8xy}{2}$

Solution:

$$\frac{20x^2y + 6xy^3 - 8xy}{2} = \frac{2(10x^2y + 3xy^3 - 4xy)}{2} = 10x^2y + 3xy^3 - 4xy$$

5. Factoring

    Factoring is the reverse process of multiplication.

    Example 1:

    Multiply: $a(b + c) = ab + ac$

    Factor: $ab + ac = a(b + c)$

    In factoring, we first factor out the greatest common factor of the terms from the polynomial.

    Example 2:

    Since the greatest common factor (GCF) of $36x^3y$, $84x^2y^2$, and $-24x^2y^4$ is $12x^2y$, we have $36x^3y + 84x^2y^2 - 24x^2y^4 = 12x^2y\,(3x + 7y - 2y^3)$, and

    $$\frac{36x^3y + 84x^2y^2 - 24x^2y^4}{12x^2y} = 3x + 7y - 2y^3.$$

6. Solution of linear equations

In solving $ax = b$, we know that the solution is $x = \dfrac{b}{a}$. If we are given a linear equation to solve which is not in the form $ax = b$, we try to express the equation in the form $ax = b$.

Example 1:

Solve: $5(x + \dfrac{1}{5}) = 16$

Solution:

$5(x + \dfrac{1}{5}) = 16$

$5(x) + 5\left(\dfrac{1}{5}\right) = 16$ by the distributive property

$5x + 1 = 16$ $\dfrac{1}{5}$ is the inverse of 5, if the operation $*$ is the usual multiplication.

$(5x + 1) + (-1) = 16 + (-1)$ If we add the same number to both sides of an equality we do not change the solution of the equality.

$5x + [1 + (-1)] = 15$ by the associative property

$5x + 0 = 15$ (-1) is the inverse of 1, if the operation $*$ is the usual addition.

$5x = 15$ since 0 is the identity element if the operation $*$ is the usual addition.

$\dfrac{1}{5}(5x) = \dfrac{1}{5}(15)$ Multiply both sides by $\dfrac{1}{5}$ to get x on the left.

$x = 3$

C. Extension of Algebraic Skills

1. Factoring

   Example 1:

   Multiply: $(x + y)(x - y) = x^2 - y^2$
   Factor: $x^2 - y^2 = (x + y)(x - y)$

   Example 2:

   Multiply: $(x + y)(x + y) = x^2 + 2xy + y^2$
   Factor: $x^2 + 2xy + y^2 = (x + y)(x + y)$

2. Simplifying algebraic fractions with polynomial denominators

   Simplifying an algebraic fraction with a polynomial denominator usually amounts to factoring both the numerator and the denominators in order to find any common factors. By common factor, we mean an algebraic expression that is a factor of both the numerator and the denominator.

   Example 1:

   Simplify: $\dfrac{x^3 + 6x^2 + 9x}{x^2 - 9}$

   Solution:

   $$\frac{x^3 + 6x^2 + 9x}{x^2 - 9} = \frac{x(x^2 + 6x + 9)}{x^2 - 3^2} =$$

   $$\frac{x(x + 3)(x + 3)}{(x - 3)(x + 3)} = \frac{x(x + 3)}{(x - 3)} \text{, if } x \neq -3.$$

3. Multiplication and division of fractions with polynomial denominators

Example 1:

Simplify: $\dfrac{x-3}{3x} \cdot \dfrac{x^3 + 6x^2 + 9x}{x^2 - 9}$

Solution:

$$\frac{x-3}{3x} \cdot \frac{x^3 + 6x^2 + 9x}{x^2 - 9} = \frac{(x-3)}{3x} \cdot \frac{x(x+3)(x+3)}{(x-3)(x+3)}$$

$$= \frac{(x-3)}{3x} \cdot \frac{x(x+3)}{(x-3)} = \frac{x+3}{3}, \text{ if } x \neq 3, -3, \text{ or } 0.$$

Example 2:

Simplify: $\dfrac{x-3}{3x} \div \dfrac{x^3 + 6x^2 + 9x}{x^2 - 9}$

Solution:

$$\frac{x-3}{3x} \div \frac{x^3 + 6x^2 + 9x}{x^2 - 9} = \frac{x-3}{3x} \div \frac{x(x+3)(x+3)}{(x-3)(x+3)}$$

$$= \frac{x-3}{3x} \div \frac{x(x+3)}{x-3}$$

$$= \frac{x-3}{3x} \times \frac{x-3}{x(x+3)}$$

$$= \frac{(x-3)^2}{3x^2(x+3)}$$

4. Addition and subtraction of fractions

Example 1:

Find the least common multiple of $3xy$, $5x^2y$, and $30y^2$.

First note that

the least common multiple of 3, 5, and 30 is 30,
the least common multiple of x and x^2 is x^2, and
the least common multiple of y and y^2 is y^2.

Therefore the least common multiple of $3xy$, $5x^2y$, and $30xy^2$ is the product $30xy^2$.

Example 2:

Add: $\dfrac{1}{3xy} + \dfrac{2}{5x^2y} - \dfrac{3}{30y^2}$

Solution:

$$\frac{1}{3xy} + \frac{2}{5x^2y} - \frac{3}{30y^2} = \frac{10xy}{30x^2y^2} + \frac{12y}{30x^2y^2} - \frac{3x^2}{30x^2y^2} =$$

$$\frac{10xy + 12y - 3x^2}{30x^2y^2}$$

D. Groups and Fields

1. Groups

    a. Definition

        A group G is a nonempty set with binary operation $*$ satisfying the following properties:

        1. G is closed under $*$, that is, $a * b$ is in G, for all a and b in G.

        2. $*$ is associative on G.

        3. Every element in G has an inverse.

        4. There is an identity element in G.

Example 1:

The set of real numbers with usual addition forms a group.

b.   Infinite systems

A set is infinite if its elements cannot be counted completely, no matter how fast we count or how much time we take.

Example 1:

The set of real numbers, the set of integers, the set of rationals, the set of irrationals are all infinite sets.

c.   Finite systems

A set is finite if it is empty or we can count the elements of the set completely.

Example 2:

Let $A = \{$all left-handed people in USA$\}$. A is a finite set.

2.   Fields

a.   Definition

Let F be a set and let $\oplus, \otimes$ be two operations on F. Then F is a field if the following conditions are satisfied:

1. F is a commutative group under the operation $\oplus$.

2.   The nonzero elements of F form a group under the operation $\otimes$.

3.   The operation $\otimes$ distributes over $\oplus$.

4.   The identity element with respect to the operation $\oplus$ is different than the identity element with respect to the operation $\otimes$.

Example 1:

The set of real numbers is a field if the operation $\oplus$ is the usual addition and the operation $\otimes$ is the usual multiplication.

Questions

In questions 1−4, refer to the table:

*	2	4	6	8
2	4	8	2	6
4	8	6	4	2
6	2	4	6	8
8	6	2	8	4

In this table the first column represents the first component and the second column represents the second component.

1. Determine $4 * 8$

2. Is the set closed under $*$? Why or why not?

3. Which element, if any, is the identity?

4. Which element, if any, is the inverse of 8?

5. If x and y are whole numbers, let's define $*$ to be $x * y = \dfrac{x+y}{2}$. Is the set of whole numbers closed under $*$?

6. Find two examples to show that the odd integers are not closed under adddition.

7. Define an operator, $*$, on $\{1, 2, 3, 4, 5\}$ such that
   - If $x \neq y$, then $x * y$ is the larger number of x and y;
   - If $x = y$, then $x * y$ is 1.

   Construct an operation table for $*$ on $\{1, 2, 3, 4, 5\}$.

8. The table defines a group. What is the identity element?

*	2	5	8
2	8	2	5
5	2	5	8
8	5	8	2

9. Perform the following operations and simplify the result.
   a. $(-5x^3 - x^2 + 1) + (3x^3 + x^2 - 3x + 2)$
   b. $(2x^3 + 2x^2 - 3x) - (x^3 - 5x^2 - 3x + 4)$
   c. $(x + y)(x - y + z)$

10. Factor the given expressions.
    a. $4x^2 - 9a^2$
    b. $3x^2 + x - 10$

11. Perform the indicated operation and simplify:

$$\frac{x+2}{2x-3y} \cdot \frac{4x^2-9y^2}{xy+2y}$$

Answers

1. 2

2. Yes, because the values of the table are all elements of the set {2, 4, 6, 8}.

3. 6 is the identity element.

4. Since $8 * 2 = 6 = 2 * 8$, 2 is the inverse of 8.

5. No. Let $x = 1$ and $y = 2$, then $x * y = \dfrac{3}{2}$, which is not a whole number.

6. $1 + 3 = 4$ which is even, $1 + 5 = 6$ which is even.

7.

*	1	2	3	4	5
1	1	2	3	4	5
2	2	1	3	4	5
3	3	3	1	4	5
4	4	4	4	1	5
5	5	5	5	5	1

8. 5 is the identity element.

9. a. $-2x^3 - 3x + 3$

   b. $x^3 + 7x^2 - 4$

   c. $x^2 + xz - y^2 + yz$

10. a. $4x^2 - 9a^2 = (2x + 3a)(2x - 3a)$

   b. $3x^2 + x - 10 = (3x - 5)(x + 2)$

11. $\dfrac{x + 2}{2x - 3y} \cdot \dfrac{4x^2 - 9y^2}{xy + 2y} =$

$\dfrac{x + 2}{2x - 3y} \cdot \dfrac{(2x - 3y)(2x + 3y)}{y(x + 2)} =$

$\dfrac{2x + 3y}{y}$.

Chapter 4

Euclidean Geometry

A. Axiomatic Systems

1. Undefined terms and definitions

In study of geometry, we accept the terms POINT, LINE, and PLANE as undefined. Except for these three undefined terms, we must define each geometric term we use. To be certain that a definition is understood, we can only use the terms that are already defined or accepted as undefined.

2. Assumptions

In addition to agreeing on certain terms without defining them, we have to agree on certain relations without proving them. These relations that we accept without proof are called the axioms or postulates of our geometric system.

3. Theorems and proof

Before accepting a conjecture into our geometric system, we must prove that it is always true in our system. To do this, we must show that it follows logically from ideas that we have already assumed or proved. Such conjectures are called theorems.

Example 1:

Let's create a system of our own.

Undefined terms: parrot, word, speak

Axioms:

1. There are exactly three parrots.

2. Every parrot speaks at least two words.

3. No word is spoken by more than two parrots.

Now, let's state a theorem and show that it follows logically from the axioms.

Theorem 1: There are at least three words.

Proof: We will give an indirect proof. Suppose the statement of the theorem is not true. Thus, assume that there are only two words. Hence by axiom 2, every parrot must speak those two words. By axiom 1, there are three parrots that speak each word, but this contradicts axiom 3. Then our assumption, there were only two words, must be wrong. Therefore, there are at least three words.

B. Congruence

Definition 1: Collinear points are points that are contained in one line.

Definition 2: Coplanar points are points that are contained in one plane.

Definition 3: A segment, $\overline{RT}$, is the set of points R and T and all the points between R and T.

Definition 4: The midpoint of $\overline{RT}$ is a point S between R and T such that $RS = ST$.

Definition 5: Two triangles are congruent, $\cong$, if they have the same size and the same shape but contain different points.

Note: The order is important. When we say $\triangle ABC \cong \triangle XYZ$, we mean that:

$\angle A \cong \angle X, \quad \overline{AB} \cong \overline{XY},$

$\angle B \cong \angle Y, \quad \overline{BC} \cong \overline{YZ},$

$\angle C \cong \angle Z, \quad \overline{AC} \cong \overline{XZ}.$

If A, B, and C are noncollinear , the union of $\overline{AB}$, $\overline{BC}$, and $\overline{AC}$ is triangle ABC, denoted by $\triangle ABC$. A, B, and C are the vertices of the triangle; $\overline{AB}$, $\overline{BC}$, and $\overline{AC}$ are its sides. $\angle A$, $\angle B$, and $\angle C$ are the angles of $\triangle ABC$.

1. Assumptions

Two triangles are congruent if any one of the following conditions hold:

SSS postulate states that if $\overline{AB} \cong \overline{XY}$, $\overline{BC} \cong \overline{YZ}$, and $\overline{AC} \cong \overline{XZ}$, then $\triangle ABC \cong \triangle XYZ$.

SAS postulate states that if $\overline{BC} \cong \overline{YZ}$, $\overline{AC} \cong \overline{XZ}$, and $\angle C \cong \angle Z$, then $\triangle ABC \cong \triangle XYZ$.

ASA postulate states that if $\overline{AB} \cong \overline{XY}$, $\angle A \cong \angle X$, and $\angle B \cong \angle Y$, then $\triangle ABC \cong \triangle XYZ$.

2. Isosceles triangle theorems

Definition 1. An isosceles triangle is one with at least two congruent sides.

Theorem 1. In an isosceles triangle, the angles opposite the two congruent sides are congruent.

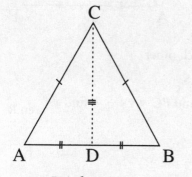

Proof:

Statements	Reasons
1. $\overline{AC} \cong \overline{BC}$	1. Given
2. Let D be the midpoint of $\overline{AB}$.	2. A segment has one and only one midpoint.
3. Draw $\overline{CD}$.	3. Two points are contained in one and only one line.
4. $AD = DB$	4. Definition of midpoint
5. $\overline{AD} \cong \overline{DB}$	5. Definition of congruence statements
6. $\overline{CD} \cong \overline{CD}$	6. Congruence of segments is reflexive.
7. $\triangle ADC \cong \triangle BDC$	7. SSS Postulate applied to steps 1, 5, and 6.
8. $\angle A \cong \angle B$	8. Corresponding parts of congruent triangles are congruent.

Theorem 2. If two angles of a triangle are congruent, then the sides opposite these angles are congruent.

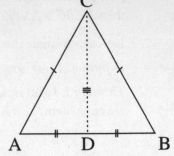

Proof:

Assume that $\angle A \cong \angle B$.

Draw $\overline{CD}$, the altitude from

C to AB. Observe that

$\triangle ACD \cong \triangle BCD$ by ASA postulate.

Then $\overline{AC} \cong \overline{BC}$.

Observe that Theorems 1 and 2 are converse of each other.

Example 1:

In the following diagram, if $\angle A \cong \angle B$, $AC = 12$, and $BC = 2x + 4$, find x.

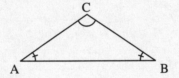

Solution:

By Theorem 2, we have $BC = AC$. Therefore, $2x + 4 = 12$. Hence $x = 4$.

3. Other congruence postulates (AAS, HL)

Besides the SSS, SAS, and ASA postulates, we have some other postulates to prove two triangles are congruent.

1. AAS postulate states that two triangles are congruent if two angles and a side opposite one of them are congruent to two angles and the corresponding side in the other.

2. HL postulate states that if the hypotenuse and a leg of one right triangle are congruent to the hypotenuse and a leg of another right triangle, the triangles are congruent.

Example 1:

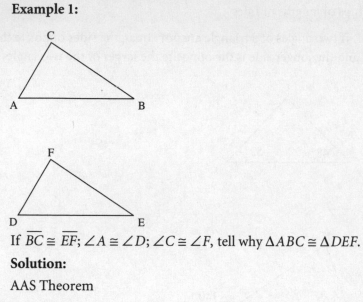

If $\overline{BC} \cong \overline{EF}$; $\angle A \cong \angle D$; $\angle C \cong \angle F$, tell why $\triangle ABC \cong \triangle DEF$.

Solution:

AAS Theorem

C. Inequalities

Theorem 1. If $a = b + c$, and c is a positive number, then $a > b$.

We basically use the above algebraic theorem to prove statements about inequalities.

1. Angle relationships

Theorem 1. If one of the sides of a triangle is extended, then the exterior angle is greater than either opposite interior angle.

Theorem 2. If two sides of a triangle are not equal, than the angles opposite them are not equal and the larger angle lies opposite the longer side.

2. Relationships of lengths of sides

   Theorem 1. If two angles of a triangle are not equal, the sides opposite them are not equal and the longer side is the opposite the larger of the two angles.

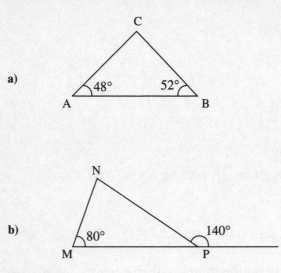

a)

b)

Example 1:

Find the longest and the shortest side in each triangle.

Solution:

Longest: a. $\overline{AB}$ b. $\overline{NP}$

Shortest: a. $\overline{BC}$ b. $\overline{MN}$

Theorem 2. The sum of the lengths of any two sides of a triangle is greater than the length of the third side.

Example 2:

Tell whether it is possible for a triangle to have sides of the given lengths.

a.   18, 10, 7

b. $2x, x, x + 1$

Solution:

a. No, since $10 + 7 < 18$

b. Yes

D. Parallelism

1. Definitions and assumptions

Parallel lines are lines that are coplanar and do not intersect. If l and m are parallel, we write l||m.

A *transversal* is a line that intersects two coplanar lines in two distinct points.

Vertical angles are angles whose sides form two pairs of opposite rays.

Two angles are *complementary* if and only if the sum of their measures is 90 degrees.

Two angles are *supplementary* if and only if the sum of their measures is 180 degrees.

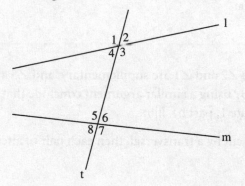

Interior angles	∠3, ∠4, ∠5, ∠6
Exterior angles	∠1, ∠2, ∠7, ∠8
Alternate interior angles	∠3 and ∠5, ∠4 and ∠6
Corresponding angles	∠1 and ∠5, ∠2 and ∠6, ∠4 and ∠8, ∠3 and ∠7

The two angles of the triangle that are not adjacent to a particular exterior angle are called the *remote interior angles* with respect to that exterior angle.

2. Theorems and Postulates

Postulate 1:

a. If two parallel lines are cut by a transversal, then each pair of corresponding angles are congruent.

b. If two lines are cut by a transversal such that each pair of corresponding angles are congruent, then the two lines are parallel.

Theorem 1. If two lines are cut by a transversal such that one pair of corresponding angles are congruent, then the lines are parallel.

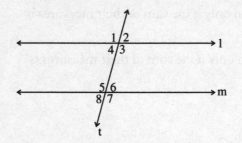

Proof: Assume that $\angle 1 \cong \angle 5$. Since $\angle 2$ and $\angle 1$ are supplementary, and $\angle 5$ and $\angle 6$ are supplementary, $\angle 2 \cong \angle 6$. By using a similar argument conclude that $\angle 4 \cong \angle 8$, and $\angle 3 \cong \angle 7$. Then by Postulate 1, part b), $l \| m$.

Theorem 2. If two parallel lines are cut by a transversal, then each pair of alternate interior angles are congruent.

Proof:

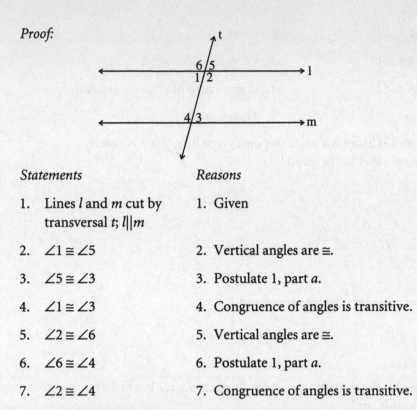

Statements	Reasons
1. Lines *l* and *m* cut by transversal *t*; *l*‖*m*	1. Given
2. ∠1 ≅ ∠5	2. Vertical angles are ≅.
3. ∠5 ≅ ∠3	3. Postulate 1, part *a*.
4. ∠1 ≅ ∠3	4. Congruence of angles is transitive.
5. ∠2 ≅ ∠6	5. Vertical angles are ≅.
6. ∠6 ≅ ∠4	6. Postulate 1, part *a*.
7. ∠2 ≅ ∠4	7. Congruence of angles is transitive.

Theorem 3. If two lines are cut by a transversal such that one pair of alternate interior angles are congruent, then the lines are parallel.

Proof:

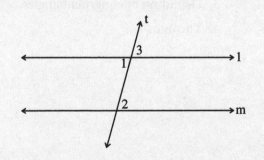

Statements	Reasons
1. Lines *l* and *m* cut by transversal *t*.	1. Given

2. $\angle 1 \cong \angle 2$ 2. Given

3. $\angle 3 \cong \angle 1$ 3. Vertical angles are $\cong$.

4. $\angle 3 \cong \angle 2$ 4. Congruence of angles is transitive.

5. $l \| m$ 5. Theorem 1

Theorem 4. Through a point not on a given line, there is exactly one line parallel to the given line.

Proof:

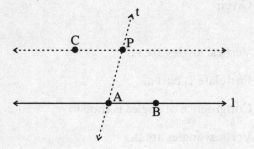

Statements	Reasons
1. Choose two points, A and B, on l.	1. A line contains at least two points.
2. Draw PA.	2. Two points are contained in one and only one line.
3. $\angle CPA \cong \angle PAB$.	3. Definition of congruent angles
4. $CP \| l$.	4. Theorem 1

Example 1:

Given: l‖m; . ∠2 ≅ ∠5 Prove: s‖t.

Solution:

Statements	Reasons
1. *l‖m*	1. Given
2. ∠3 ≅ ∠2	2. Theorem 2
3. ∠2 ≅ ∠5	3. Given
4. ∠3 ≅ ∠5	4. Transitivity
5. *s‖t*	5. Theorem 1

3. Angle measure in triangles

   A *right angle* is an angle whose measure is 90°. An *acute angle* is one whose measure is less than 90°. An *obtuse angle* is one whose measure is greater than 90°.

   1. The acute angles of a right triangle are complementary.

   2. The degree measure of each acute angle of an isosceles right triangle is 45°.

   3. The degree measure of each angle of an equilateral triangle is 60°.

4. The measure of an exterior angle of a triangle is equal to the sum of the measures of the two remote interior angles.

5. The sum of the measures of the angles of a quadrilateral is 360°.

4. Classification and properties of quadrilaterals

A *parallelogram* is a quadrilateral with two pairs of opposite sides parallel.

A *trapezoid* is a quadrilateral in which exactly one pair of opposite sides is parallel.

A *rhombus* is a parallelogram with four congruent sides.

Theorem 1. A diagonal and the sides of a parallelogram form two congruent triangles.

Proof:

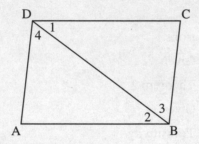

Statements	Reasons
1. *ABCD* is a parallelogram with diagonal $\overline{DB}$.	1. Given
2. $\overline{DB} \cong \overline{DB}$	2. Congruence of segments is reflexive.
3. $\overline{AB} \parallel \overline{DC}$; $\overline{AD} \parallel \overline{CB}$	3. Definition of parallelogram
4. $\angle 1 \cong \angle 2$; $\angle 3 \cong \angle 4$	4. Section D, Part 2, Theorem 2.
5. $\triangle ABD \cong \triangle CDB$	5. ASA Postulate

Theorem 2: The diagonals of a parallelogram bisect each other.

Proof:

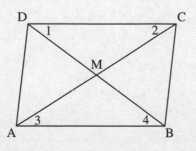

Statements	*Reasons*
1. *ABCD* is a parallelogram with diagonals $\overline{AC}$ and $\overline{BD}$.	1. Given
2. $\overline{AB} \cong \overline{CD}$	2. Opposite sides of a parallelogram are congruent
3. $\overline{AB} \parallel \overline{CD}$	3. Definition of a parallelogram
4. $\angle 1 \cong \angle 4; \angle 3 \cong \angle 2$	4. Section D, Part 2, Theorem 2
5. $\triangle AMB \cong \triangle CMD$	5. ASA Postulate
6. $\overline{AM} \cong \overline{CM}; \overline{DM} \cong \overline{BM}$	6. Corresponding parts of congruent triangles are $\cong$
7. $AM = CM; DM = BM$	7. Definition of $\cong$ segments
8. *M* is the midpoint of both $\overline{AC}$ and $\overline{DB}$	8. Definition of midpoint
9. $\overline{AC}$ and $\overline{DB}$ bisect each other.	9. Definition of bisect

Theorem 3. If two sides of a quadrilateral are parallel and congruent, then the quadrilateral is a parallelogram.

Proof:

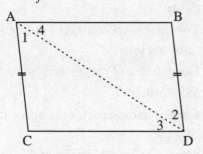

Statements	*Reasons*
1. *ABCD* is a quadrilateral.	1. Given
2. $\overline{AD} \cong \overline{CB}; \overline{AD} \parallel \overline{CB}$	2. Given
3. Draw $\overline{AC}$	3. Two points are contained in one and only one line.
4. $\overline{AC} \cong \overline{AC}$	4. Congruence of segments is reflexive.
5. $\angle 1 \cong \angle 2$	5. Section D, Part 2, Theorem 2

6. $\triangle ACB \cong \triangle CAD$	6. SAS Postulate
7. $\angle 3 \cong \angle 4$	7. Corresponding parts of congruent triangles are $\cong$
8. $\overline{AB} \parallel \overline{DC}$	8. Section D, Part 2, Theorem 3
9. $ABCD$ is a parallelogram.	9. Definition of parallelogram

Theorem 4. If both pairs of opposite sides of a quadrilateral are congruent, then the quadrilateral is a parallelogram.

Proof:

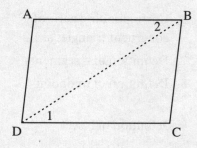

Statements	Reasons
1. $ABCD$ is a quadrilateral.	1. Given
2. $\overline{AB} \cong \overline{CD}$; and $\overline{BC} \cong \overline{DA}$	2. Given
3. Draw $\overline{BD}$	3. Two points are contained in one and only one line.
4. $\overline{BD} \cong \overline{BD}$	4. Congruence of segments is reflexive.
5. $\triangle ABD \cong \triangle CDB$	5. SSS Postulate
6. $\angle 1 \cong \angle 2$	6. Corresponding parts of congruent triangles are $\cong$.
7. $\overline{AB} \parallel \overline{CD}$	7. Section D, Part 2, Theorem 3
8. $ABCD$ is a parallelogram.	8. Theorem 3

Properties of quadrilaterals:

1. The opposite angles of a parallelogram are congruent.

2. If the diagonals of a quadrilateral bisect each other, then the quadrilateral is a parallelogram.

3. The diagonals of a rhombus are perpendicular.

4. The diagonals of a rectangle are congruent.

5. The diagonals of a rhombus bisect the angles of the rhombus.

6. The base angles of an isosceles trapezoid are congruent.

7. The diagonals of an isosceles trapezoid are congruent.

E. Similarity

1. Definition of similar polygons

Two polygons are similar, ~, if there is a one-to-one correspondence between their vertices such that corresponding angles are congruent, and the ratios of the lengths of corresponding sides are equal.

2. Similar triangles

AA Postulate states that if two angles of one triangle are congruent to two angles of another, the triangles are similar.

Theorem 1. If the lengths of the sides of one triangle are proportional to the lengths of the sides of a second triangle, the triangles are similar.

Theorem 2. If a line parallel to one side of a triangle intersects the other two sides, it divides them proportionally.

Theorem 3. If a line segment connects the midpoints of two sides of a triangle, it is parallel to the third side and has a length half of the length of the third side.

Theorem 4. If an altitude is drawn to the hypotenuse of a right triangle, the new triangles formed are similar to each other and to the given triangle.

Definition: The geometric mean of two positive real numbers, a and b, is the positive number x such that $\frac{a}{x} = \frac{x}{b}$. Note that this can also be expressed as $x = \sqrt{ab}$.

Theorem 5. The length of the altitude to the hypotenuse of a right triangle is the geometric mean of the lengths of the segments into which the altitude separates the hypotenuse.

Theorem 6. If the altitude to the hypotenuse is drawn in a right triangle, the length of either leg is the geometric mean of the lengths of the hypotenuse and the segment on the hypotenuse which is adjacent to that leg.

Example 1. Find h.

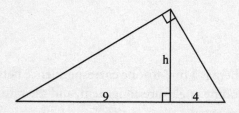

Solution:

By Theorem 5, $h^2 = 9(4) = 36$. Therefore, $h = 6$.

Example 2. Find b.

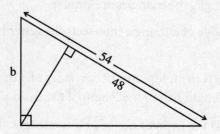

Solution:

By Theorem 6, $b^2 = 54(54 - 48) = 324$. Therefore, $b = 18$.

Example 3. Find m.

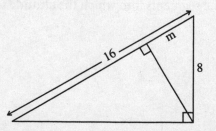

Solution:

By Theorem 6, $8^2 = 16m$. Therefore, $m = 4$.

Example 4. Find c.

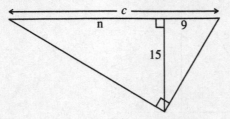

Solution:

By Theorem 5, $15^2 = 9n$. Therefore, $n = 25$. Hence $c = 9 + n = 9 + 25 = 34$.

Example 5. In the following diagram, list all pairs of similar triangles.

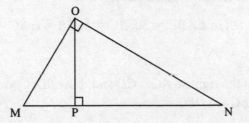

Solution:

By Theorem 4,

$\triangle OMP$, $\triangle NMO$;

$\triangle NOP$, $\triangle NMO$;

$\triangle OMP$, $\triangle NOP$.

3. Pythagorean relationship

    The Pythagorean Theorem: The square of the hypotenuse of a right triangle is equal to the sum of the squares of its legs.

4. Special right triangles

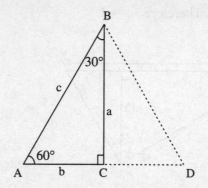

Theorem 1. In a 30-60-90 triangle, the length of the leg opposite the 30° angle is half the length of the hypotenuse, and the length of the leg opposite the angle 60° angle is $\sqrt{3}$ times the length of the other leg.

Given: $\triangle ABC$; m$\angle A = 60$; m$\angle ABC = 30$; $AC = b$; $AB = c$; $BC = a$

Prove: $b = \dfrac{1}{2}c$ and $a = b\sqrt{3}$

Proof: Extend AC to the right so $AC = CD$ and draw BD. Conclude that $\triangle ABD$ is equilateral and $\triangle ABC \cong \triangle DBC$.

Then $b = \dfrac{1}{2}c$. Apply the Pythagorean Theorem, using $2b = c$, to obtain $a = b\sqrt{3}$.

Theorem 2. In a 45-45-90 triangle, the length of the hypotenuse is $\sqrt{2}$ times the length of a leg.

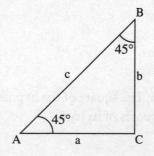

Given: Right triangle $\triangle ABC$; $m\angle A = m\angle B = 45$; $AB = c$; $AC = b$.

Prove: $c = a\sqrt{2}$.

Proof: Use Theorem 2 from section B.2, isosceles triangle theorem, to conclude that $BC = a$. Then, use the Pythagorean Theorem to show that $c = a\sqrt{2}$.

5. Right triangle trigonometry

$$\sin A = \frac{\text{length of side opposite } \angle A}{\text{length of hypotenuse}}$$

$$\cos A = \frac{\text{length of side adjacent to } \angle A}{\text{length of hypotenuse}}$$

$$\tan A = \frac{\text{length of side opposite } \angle A}{\text{length of side adjacent to } \angle A}$$

F. Constructions and Proofs

1. Basic constructions

By using only a straightedge and compass, we can

1. Construct a line segment congruent to a given line segment

2. Construct an angle congruent to a given angle

3. Construct a perpendicular bisector of a given line segment

4. Bisect a given angle

5. Construct a perpendicular to a given line from a given point not on the line

6. Construct a perpendicular to a given line from a given point on the line

7. Construct a line parallel to a given line through a given point not on the given line

Note that we can justify some of the above basic constructions by using similar, and congruent triangles.

Questions

1.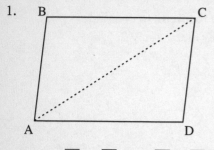

Given $\overline{AD} \cong \overline{CB}$, and $\overline{AB} \cong \overline{CD}$, prove that $\triangle ABC \cong \triangle CDA$.

2.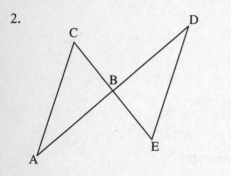

Given: B is the midpoint of $\overline{AD}$ and $\overline{CE}$

Prove: $\triangle ABC \cong \triangle DBE$.

3.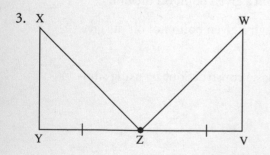

Given: $\angle XZY \cong \angle WZV$; Z is the midpoint of $\overline{YV}$; $\angle Y$ and $\angle V$ are right angles.

Prove : $\triangle XYZ \cong \triangle WVZ$.

4.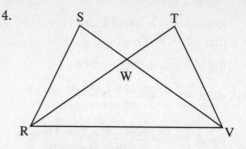

Name the two triangles you would prove congruent, in order to prove each statement.

a. $\overline{RT} \cong \overline{VS}$
b. $\overline{RW} \cong \overline{VW}$

5.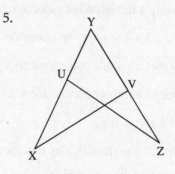

Decide if the large triangles xyv and uyz are congruent, and give reasons for each case.

a. $\overline{XY} \cong \overline{ZY}$; $\overline{YU} \cong \overline{YV}$
b. $\angle X \cong \angle Z$; $\overline{XV} \cong \overline{ZU}$
c. $\angle X \cong \angle Z$; $\overline{XY} \cong \overline{ZY}$.

6. Decide if it is possible for a triangle to have sides of the given lengths. Assume x is greater than 2.

   a. 9, 7, 14
   b. $x, 2, x - 2$

7. In the following parallelogram,

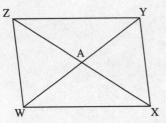

   a. If $ZY = 7x + 5$, and $WX = 4x + 17$, find x.
   b. If $m\angle WZY = 10y + 7$ and $m\angle WXY = 8y + 25$, find y.
   c. If $AW = 3a$ and $WY - 3a + 18$, find a.
   d. If $m\angle ZWX = 4x + 7$ and $m\angle WXY = 6x + 3$, find $m\angle WXY$.

8.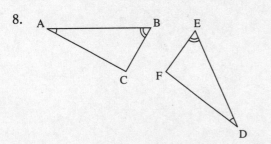

   Given $\triangle ABC$ and $\triangle DEF$, $\angle A \cong \angle D$; $\angle B \cong \angle E$, supply the missing terms.

   a. $\dfrac{AB}{DE} = \dfrac{BC}{?}$

   b. $\dfrac{DE}{AB} = \dfrac{DF}{?}$

9.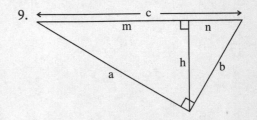

   Find the indicated lengths.

   a. $m = 3; c = 12; a = ?$
   b. $n = 4; c = 9; b = ?$
   c. $m = 28; n = 7; h = ?$
   d. $m = 25; n = 4; h = ?$

10. Which of the following represent lengths of sides of a right triangle?

    a. 4, 5, and 7
    b. 20, 21, and 29
    c. 9, 40 and 41
    d. 9, 12, and 16

11. In △*ABC*, which trigonometric ratio is represented for the given angle?

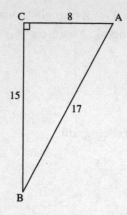

   a. $\dfrac{15}{8}$, ∠*A*

   b. $\dfrac{8}{17}$, ∠*A*

   c. $\dfrac{15}{17}$, ∠*A*

   d. $\dfrac{8}{17}$, ∠*B*

   e. $\dfrac{8}{15}$, ∠*B*

   f. $\dfrac{15}{17}$, ∠*B*

Answers

1. *Statements*

$\overline{AD} \cong \overline{CB}$, and $\overline{AB} \cong \overline{CD}$

$\overline{AC} \cong \overline{CA}$

$\triangle ABC \cong \triangle CDA$

Reasons

Given

Congruence of segments is reflexive.

SSS postulate

2. *Statements*

B is the midpoint of $\overline{AD}$ and $\overline{CE}$.

$AB = BD$, and $CB = BE$

$\overline{AB} \cong \overline{BD}$, $\overline{CB} \cong \overline{BE}$

$\angle ABC \cong \angle DBE$

$\triangle ABC \cong \triangle DBE$

Reasons

Given

Definition of midpoint

Definition of congruent segments

Vertical angles are congruent

SAS postulate

3. *Statements*

1. $\angle XZY \cong \angle WZV$
2. Z is the midpoint of $\overline{YV}$.
3. $YZ = ZV$
4. $\overline{YZ} \cong \overline{ZV}$
5. $\angle Y$ and $\angle V$ are right angles.
6. $\angle Y \cong \angle V$
7. $\triangle XYZ \cong \triangle WVZ$

Reasons

1. Given
2. Given
3. Definition of midpoint
4. Definition of congruent segments
5. Given

6. Right angles are congruent.
7. ASA postulate

4. a. $\triangle RTV \cong \triangle VSR$
   b. $\triangle RSW \cong \triangle VTW$

5. a. Congruent, SAS postulate
   b. Congruent, AAS postulate
   c. Congruent, ASA postulate

6. a. Yes
   b. No, observe that $(x - 2) + 2$ cannot be greater than the third side, x.

7. a. Since $ZY = WX$, $x = 4$.
   b. Since m$\angle WZY \cong$ m$\angle WXY$, $y = 9$.
   c. Since $WY = 2\,AW$, $a = 6$.
   d. Since m$\angle ZWX +$ m$\angle WXY = 180$, we have $x = 17$. Therefore, m$\angle WXY = 6x + 3 = 105$.

8. Observe that $\triangle ABC \cong \triangle DEF$. Therefore, the ratios of the lengths of corresponding sides are equal.
   a. EF
   b. AC

9. a. 6
   b. 6
   c. 14
   d. 10

10. a. No
    b. Yes
    c. Yes
    d. No

11. a. $\tan A$
    b. $\cos A$
    c. $\sin A$
    d. $\sin B$
    e. $\tan B$
    f. $\cos B$

Chapter 5

Analytic Geometry

A. Review of the Rectangular Coordinate System

The x–axis and y–axis are perpendicular number lines. They meet at the origin, a point corresponding to zero on both lines. A point is located by an ordered pair of real numbers.

Example 1:

The x-coordinate of the point $(-2, 3)$ is -2, and y-coordinate is 3. The x-coordinate, -2, means that $(-2, 3)$ is located on a vertical line two units to the left of the y-axis. The y-coordinate, 3, means that $(-2, 3)$ is located on a horizontal line three units above the x-axis.

The *slope*, m, of a nonvertical line that contains two points (x_1, y_1) and (x_2, y_2) is $m = \dfrac{y_2 - y_1}{x_2 - x_1}$.

B. Parallel and Perpendicular Lines

1. Parallel lines

Two nonvertical lines are parallel if they have equal slopes. The converse statement is also true; if two lines have equal slopes, they are parallel.

2. Perpendicular lines

Two nonvertical lines are perpendicular if and only if their slopes are the negative reciprocals of each other.

Example 1:

Decide if the points $(9, -2)$, $(4, 5)$, and $(11, 10)$ are vertices of a right triangle.

Solution: Observe that the slope of the line passing through

$(4, 5)$, and $(11, 10)$ is $\dfrac{5}{7}$, and the slope of the line passing through

$(9, -2)$, and $(4, 5)$ is $-\dfrac{7}{5}$. Therefore, the answer is yes.

C. Formulas

1. Length of a segment

    When a segment is parallel to the x-axis, its length is found by finding the positive difference of the x-coordinates. Thus, if the endpoints of the line segment are (x_1, y_1) and (x_2, y_1), then the length of the line segment is $x_2 - x_1$, or $x_1 - x_2$, whichever is positive. Similarly, when a line segment is parallel to the y-axis, its length is found by finding the positive difference of the y-coordinates. Thus, if the endpoints of the line segment are (x_1, y_1) and (x_1, y_2), then the length of the line segment is $y_2 - y_1$, or $y_1 - y_2$, whichever is positive.

    In general, if (x_1, y_1) and (x_2, y_2) are end points of a line segment, then the length of the line segment, d, is given by $\sqrt{(x_2 - x_1)^2 + (y_2 - y_1)^2}$.

    Example 1:

    Show that the points $(0, -3)$, $(-2, 1)$, and $(4, -1)$ are the vertices of an isosceles triangle.

    Solution:

    The distance between $(0, -3)$ and $(-2, 1)$ is $\sqrt{(-2 - 0)^2 + [1 - (-3)]^2} = \sqrt{20}$, and the distance between $(0, -3)$ and $(4, -1)$ is also $\sqrt{(4 - 0)^2 + (-1 - (-3))^2} = \sqrt{20}$.

2. Midpoint of a segment

    The coordinates of the midpoint of a line segment with endpoints (x_1, y_1) and (x_2, y_2) are $\left(\dfrac{x_1 + x_2}{2}, \dfrac{y_1 + y_2}{2} \right)$.

D. Equation of a Line

1. Point-slope form

    If m is the slope of a line and (x_1, y_1) is a point on the line, the equation of the line is given as $y - y_1 = m(x - x_1)$.

2. Slope-intercept form

    If we are given the slope, m, and y-intercept, b, of a line, then the equation of the line is $y = mx + b$.

    Example 1:

    Find n so that a line containing $(5, -2)$ and $(-4, n)$ has the slope 1.

Solution: The slope $m = \dfrac{n - (-2)}{-4 - 5} = \dfrac{n + 2}{-9} = 1$ implies that $n = -11$.

Example 2:

Write an equation of the line containing $(6, 2)$ with slope $m = \dfrac{3}{4}$.

Solution:

$y - 2 = \dfrac{3}{4}(x - 6)$

Example 3:

Write an equation of the line with slope -2 and y-intercept -3.

Solution:

$y = -2x - 3$.

Example 4:

Write an equation of the line containing $(3, 2)$ and $(5, 1)$.

Solution: $y - 2 - -\dfrac{1}{2}(x - 3)$.

E. Area

1. Review of formulas

The *area of a square* is equal to the square of the length of a side. The *area of a rectangle* is equal to the product of the height and the width. The *area of a parallelogram* is equal to the product of the lengths of a base and the corresponding altitude. The *area of a trapezoid* is equal to one-half the product of the length of an altitude and the sum of the lengths of the bases. The *area of a triangle* is equal to one-half the product of the lengths of any side and the altitude to that side.

2. Application to coordinate geometry

Example 1:

Find the area enclosed when $(1,0)$, $(6, 0)$, $(5, 5)$, and $(2, 5)$ are joined in order.

Solution:

The enclosed region is a trapezoid. The length of the altitude is 5, and the sum of the lengths of the bases is 5 + 3. Therefore, the area is $\frac{1}{2}$ (5) (5 + 3) = 20 square units.

F.   Transformations

1.   Reflection in a line

In a plane, a reflection over a line l is a transformation that maps each point A' of the plane onto a point as follows:

- If A is on l, then $A = A'$.
- If A is not on l, then l is perpendicular bisector of $\overline{AA'}$.

Example 1:

What are the coordinates of the image of the point (a, b) if l is the

i. y-axis

ii. x-axis

iii. $y = x$

Solution:

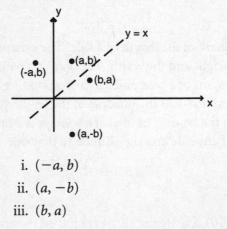

i. $(-a, b)$

ii. $(a, -b)$

iii. (b, a)

2. Reflection in a point

   If A' is the image of A under a reflection in the point P, then P is the midpoint of $\overline{AA'}$.

   Example 1:

   What are the coordinates of the image of the point (a, b) under the reflection in the origin?

   Solution:

   $(-a, -b)$

3. Translations

   The image of the point (x, y) after translating a units in the horizontal or x direction, and b units in the vertical or y direction is $(x + a, y + b)$.

   Example 1:

   A translation maps $(-1, 3)$ to $(2, 3)$. Give the coordinates of the translation image of each of the following points.

   a. $(0, 0)$

   b. $(-4, 2)$

   Solution:

   Observe that the image of a point (a, b) under translation is $(a + 3, b)$.

   a. $(3, 0)$

   b. $(-1, 2)$

4. Dilations

Let c be a real number. A dilation of (x, y) with respect to the origin is (cx, cy).

Example 1:

Let $c = 3$. Find the dilation of $(4, 8)$.

Solution:

The dilation of $(4, 8)$ is $(12, 24)$ if $c = 3$.

G. Conics

1. Circle

The equation $(x - h)^2 + (y - k)^2 = r^2$ represents a circle centered at (h, k) with radius r.

Example 1:

Let C be a circle centered at $(1, 2)$ with radius 5. Tell if the following points are interior points, exterior points, or on the circle.

a. $(4, 1)$

b. $(6, 2)$

c. $(7, 1)$

Solution:

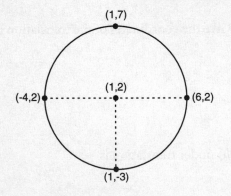

a. interior

b. on the circle

c. exterior

2. Parabola

   The equation $y = ax^2 + bx + c$ represents a parabola that is symmetric with respect to the line $x = -\dfrac{b}{2a}$.

3. Graphic solution of systems of equations

   Example 1:

   Solve: $y = x^2 + 3x + 3$ and $y = x + 2$.

   Solution:

   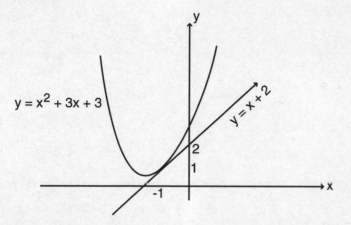

   We must have $y = x^2 + 3x + 3 = x + 2$.

   Then $x^2 + 2x + 1 = (x + 1)^2 = 0$.

   This implies that $x = -1$.

   Therefore, the solution is $(-1, 1)$.

H. Locus

1. Definition

   A *locus* is the set of all points, and only those points, that satisfy a given condition, or conditions.

   Example 1:

   In a plane, graph the locus of points equidistant from two given points, *A* and *B*.

   Solution:

   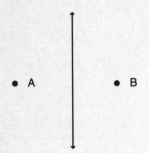

2. Basic loci

   Example 1:

   In a plane, describe the locus of points

   a. At a fixed distance from a point

   b. At a fixed distance from a line

   c. Equidistant from two points

   Description:

   a. The locus is a circle centered at the given point and with a radius of the fixed distance.

   b. The locus is a pair of lines, each the fixed distance from the given line and parallel to the given line.

   c. The locus is a line which is the perpendicular bisector of the segment joining the given points.

I.   Analytic Proof

Example 1:

Prove that if the diagonals of a rhombus are congruent, then the rhombus is a square.

Proof:

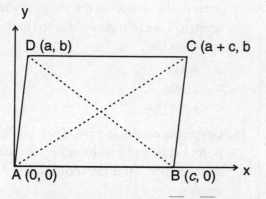

Give rhombus $ABCD$ with $\overline{AC} \cong \overline{BD}$. Place rhombus $ABCD$ on a coordinate plane so that the vertices are $A(0, 0)$, $B(c, 0)$, $D(a, b)$, and $C(a + c, b)$. We are given $\overline{AC} = \overline{BD}$. This implies $\sqrt{(a + c)^2 + b^2} = \sqrt{(a - c)^2 + b^2}$. Simplify this expression to show that $4ac = 0$. Since B is not at the origin, $c \neq 0$. Therefore $a = 0$, and the slope of $\overline{AD}$, $\dfrac{b}{a}$, is undefined. Thus $\overline{AD}$ is vertical, so $\overline{AD} \perp \overline{AB}$ and $ABCD$ is a square.

Questions

1. Find n so that a line containing $(3, n)$ and $(8, 1)$ has the slope -2.

2. Write an equation of the line containing $(1, 4)$ with slope $m = \frac{1}{2}$.

3. Write an equation of the line containing $(5, 7)$ with slope $m = -\frac{1}{4}$.

4. Write an equation of the line with slope -5, and y-intercept 8.

5. Write an equation of the line containing $(3, 3)$ and $(5, 1)$.

6. Write an equation of the line containing $(3, 5)$ and $(2, 3)$.

7. Write an equation of the line that contains the origin and is parallel to the line whose equation is $y = \frac{2}{3x + 6}$.

8. Write an equation of the line that contains the origin and is perpendicular to the line whose equation is $y = -5x - 9$.

9. Find the area enclosed when $(1, -1)$, $(5, 3)$, $(2, 5)$, and $(1, 3)$ are joined in order.

10. The triangle ABC has coordinates $(1, 0)$, $(2, 0)$, and $(2, 5)$. What are the coordinates of the vertices of the image of the triangle if the triangle is reflected in the line l and if l is the

    a. y-axis
    b. x-axis
    c. $y = x$

11. Graph the equation $y = 4$. Then graph each point below and find its reflection image over this line. State the coordinates of the images.

    a. $(5, 2)$
    b. $(-2, 4)$

12. A translation maps $(-5, 3)$ to $(-5, 7)$. Give the coordinates of the translation image of each of the following points.

    a. $(2, 0)$
    b. $(-2, -3)$

Answers

1. The slope $m = \dfrac{1-n}{8-3} = -2$. This implies

   that $\dfrac{1-n}{5} = -2$. Therefore, $1 - n = -10$,

   and hence $n = 11$.

2. Use the point-slope formula to get,

   $y - 4 = \dfrac{1}{2}(x - 1)$.

3. Use the point-slope formula to get,

   $y - 7 = -\dfrac{1}{4}(x - 5)$

4. Use the slope-intercept formula to get
   $y = -5x + 8$.

5. First observe that the slope $m = \dfrac{1-3}{5-3} = -1$.

   Then use point-slope formula to get,
   $y - 3 = -(x - 3)$.

6. First observe that the slope $m = \dfrac{3-5}{2-3} = 2$

   Then use the point-slope formula to get
   $y - 5 = 2(x - 3)$.

7. Since the line is parallel to the given line, it

   has to have the same slope, $m = \dfrac{2}{3}$. Then

   the equation of the line passing through

   $(0, 0)$ with slope $m = \dfrac{2}{3}$ is $y = \dfrac{2}{3}x$.

8. Since the line is perpendicular to the given

   line, its slope is $m = \dfrac{1}{5}$. Then the equation

   of the line passing through $(0, 0)$ with

   slope $m = \dfrac{1}{5}$ is $y = \dfrac{1}{5}x$.

9.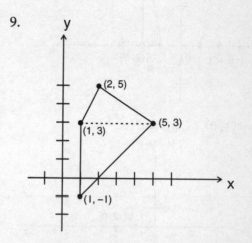

The area of the enclosed region is the sum
of the areas of two triangles. The area of one
triangle is 4 and the area of the other one is
8, so the sum is 12.

10. a. $(-1, 0), (-2, 0),$ and $(-2, 5).$

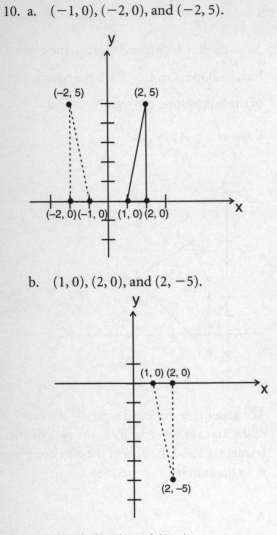

(−2, 5)   (2, 5)

(−2, 0)(−1, 0) (1, 0)(2, 0)

b. $(1, 0), (2, 0),$ and $(2, -5).$

(1, 0) (2, 0)

(2, −5)

c. $(0, 1), (0, 2),$ and $(5, 2).$

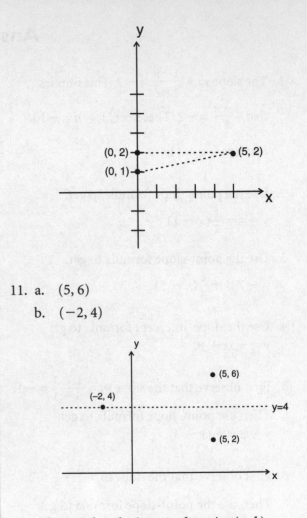

(0, 2)   (5, 2)
(0, 1)

11. a. $(5, 6)$

b. $(-2, 4)$

(5, 6)

(−2, 4)   y=4

(5, 2)

12. Observe that the image of a point (a, b) under the transformation is $(a, b + 4).$

a. The image of $(2, 0)$ is $(2, 4).$

b. The image of $(-2, -3)$ is $(-2, 1).$

Chapter 6

Equations and Inequalities

A. Review

  1. Linear equations and inequalities

    Example 1:

    Solve $7 + 3y = 1 - (3 - 5y)$

    Solution:

$7 + 3y = 1 - (3 - 5y)$	Given
$7 + 3y = 1 - 3 + 5y$	Distributive property
$7 + 3y = -2 + 5y$	Combining like terms
$7 + 3y - 5y = -2 + 5y - 5y$	Add $-5y$ to both sides.
$7 - 2y = -2$	Combining like terms.
$7 - 2y - 7 = -2 - 7$	Subtract 7 from both sides.
$-2y = -9$	Combining like terms
$y = \dfrac{9}{2}$	Multiply both sides by $-\dfrac{1}{2}$.

Properties of Inequalities:

   i. If $a < b$ and $b < c$, then $a < c$.

  ii. If $a < b$, then $a + c < b + c$.

 iii. If $a < b$ and $c > 0$, then $a \cdot c < b \cdot c$

    If $a < b$ and $c < 0$, then $a \cdot c > b \cdot c$

Example 2:

Solution:

Solve $-2x + 6 < 18 + 4x$.

$-2x + 6 < 18 + 4x$	Given
$-6x + 6 < 18$	Add $-4x$
$-6x < 12$	Add -6
$x > -2$	Multiply by $-\frac{1}{6}$, property iii, when $c < 0$.

2. Proportions

Example 1:

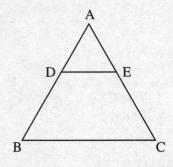

Given $\triangle ABC \sim \triangle ADE$, if

a. $AD = 9$; $AE = 6$; $AB = 15$; then $AC = ?$

b. $AE = 12$; $AC = 15$; $AB = 30$; then $AD = ?$

c. $EC = 2$; $AC = 8$; $AB = 24$; then $AD = ?$

Solution:

a.   Since $\dfrac{AD}{AE} = \dfrac{AB}{AC}$, $AC = 10$.

b.   Since $\dfrac{AD}{AB} = \dfrac{AE}{AC}$, $AD = 24$.

c.   Since $\dfrac{EC}{AC} = \dfrac{DB}{AB}$, $DB = 6$, and hence $AD = AB - DB = 24 - 6 = 18$.

B. Fractional Equations

Example 1:

Solve for x: $\frac{2}{5} + \frac{1}{x} = 15$.

Solution:

$\frac{2}{5} + \frac{1}{x} = 15$	Given
$5x\left(\frac{2}{5} + \frac{1}{x}\right) = 5x(15)$	Multiplying both sides by $5x$
$2x + 5 = 75x$	Using the distributive law on the left side and multiplying out the right side
$73x = 5$	Subtract $2x$ from both sides.
$x = \frac{5}{73}$	Divide both sides by 73.

C. Quadratic Equations

1. Solution by factoring

   Recall that:

   i. $x^2 + 2bx + b^2 = (x + b)^2$

   ii. $x^2 - a^2 = (x - a)(x + a)$

   Example 1:

   Solve $7x^2 + 19x = 6$ by factoring.

   Solution:

$7x^2 + 19x = 6$	Given
$7x^2 + 19x - 6 = 0$	Subtract 6 from both sides.
$(7x - 2)(x + 3) = 0$	Factor
$7x - 2 = 0$ or $x + 3 = 0$	If $ab = 0$, then $a = 0$ or $b = 0$.
$x = \frac{2}{7}$ or $x = -3$.	Solve for x.

Example 2:

Solve $x^2 - 9 = 0$ by factoring.

Solution:

$x^2 - 9 = 0$	Given
$(x - 3)(x + 3) = 0$	$a^2 - b^2 = (a - b)(a + b)$
$x - 3 = 0$, or $x + 3 = 0$	If $ab = 0$, then $a = 0$ or $b = 0$.
$x = 3$ or $x = -3$	Solve for x.

2. Solution by completing the square

Any expression of the form $x^2 + px$ becomes a perfect square when $\left(\dfrac{p}{2}\right)^2$ is added, since $x^2 + px + \left(\dfrac{p}{2}\right)^2 = \left(x + \dfrac{p}{2}\right)^2$.

Example 1:

Solve the quadratic equation $x^2 = 6x - 8$ by completing the square.

Solution:

$x^2 = 6x - 8$	
$x^2 - 6x = -8$	Subtract $6x$ from both sides.
$x^2 - 6x + 9 = -8 + 9$	Add $\left(\dfrac{p}{2}\right)^2 = \left(\dfrac{-6}{2}\right)^2 = (-3)^2$ to both sides.
$x^2 - 6x + 9 = 1$	Left hand side is of the form $x^2 + px + \left(\dfrac{p}{2}\right)^2$.
$(x - 3) = \pm 1$	Take the square root of both sides.
$x = 3 \pm 1$	Solve for x.
$x = 4$ or $x = 2$.	

3. Solution by quadratic formula

   If $ax^2 + bx + c = 0$, then $x = \dfrac{-b \pm \sqrt{b^2 - 4ac}}{2a}$.

   Example 1:

   Use the quadratic formula to solve $3x^2 + 4x = 4$.

   Solution:

   $3x^2 + 4x = 4$

   $3x^2 + 4x - 4 = 0$

   Here $a = 3$, $b = 4$, and $c = -4$. Thus,

   $$x = \frac{-4 \pm \sqrt{4^2 - 4(3)(-4)}}{2(3)}$$

   $$x = \frac{-4 \pm \sqrt{16 + 48}}{6}$$

   $$x = \frac{-4 \pm \sqrt{64}}{6}$$

   $$x = \frac{-4 \pm 8}{6}$$

   Therefore, $x = \dfrac{2}{3}$ or $x = -2$.

4. Applications

   Example 1:

   A gardener wants the width of his rectangular-shaped garden to be 10 meters less than half its length and wants the area of the garden to be large enough to contain 4,000 square meters. Find the dimensions of his garden.

Solution:

Let L represent the length of the garden in meters. Then the width is given by $\frac{1}{2}L - 10$. Since the area of a rectangle is the product of its length and width, we have the quadratic equation

$$L\left(\frac{1}{2}L - 10\right) = 4{,}000$$

$$\frac{1}{2}L^2 - 10L - 4{,}000 = 0$$

$$(L - 100)\left(\frac{1}{2}L + 40\right) = 0$$

Therefore, $L = 100$ or $L = -80$. But since the length of the garden can not be negative,

$L = -80$ is not a solution.

Then $L = 100$, and the width is $\frac{1}{2}L - 10 = 40$.

Example 2:

Suppose the profit P of selling x bicycles is given by $P = 24x - x^2$. How many bicycles must be sold to earn a profit of $80?

Solution:

Solve $24x - x^2 = 80$, to see that selling either 4 or 20 bicycles will yield a profit of $80.

D. Pairs of equations

1. Review of pairs of linear equations

    Example 1:

    Solve:

    $4x + 5y = 7$

    $4x + y = -5$

    Solution:

    Method I:

    If the corresponding sides of the second equation $4x + y = -5$, are subtracted from the first equation, $4x + 5y = 7$, the x terms will cancel and an equation with just the variable y will result. So $(4x + 5y) - (4x + y) = 7 - (-5)$, $4x + 5y - 4x - y = 12$, $4y = 12$, and $y = 3$. Now plug 3 for y into either original equation and solve for x. The second equation, $4x + y = -5$, will be used here because it appears to be a little easier to work with. Then $4x + 3 = -5$, $4x = -8$, and $x = -2$. Therefore the solution is $x = -2$ and $y = 3$.

    Method II:

    Solve the second equation, $4x + y = -5$, for y to get $y = -4x - 5$. Now substitute $-4x - 5$ for y in the first equation, $4x + 5y = 7$. Then $4x + 5(-4x - 5) = 7$, $4x - 20x - 25 = 7$, $-16x = 32$, $x = -2$. Now substitue -2 for x into either original equation and solve for y. The second equation $4x + y = -5$, will be used here because it appears to be a little easier to work with. Then $4(-2) + y = -5$, $-8 + y = -5$, and $y = 3$.

2. Quadratic-linear pair

Example 1:

Solve the system:

$y = x^2 + 5x + 5$

$y = x + 1$

Solution:

$y = x^2 + 5x + 5 = x + 1$	Since both of the expressions are equal to y, they must be equal.
$x^2 + 4x + 4 = 0$	Subtract $x + 1$ from to both sides.
$(x + 2)^2 = 0$	Factor.
$x = -2$	Solve for x.
$y = -1$	Solve for y.

Questions

1. Solve

   a. $9y + 7 = 4y - 3$
   b. $3(x + 2) - 1 = x - 2(1 - 3x)$

2. Solve

   a. $3(y - 2) + 5 > -2y + 4$
   b. $4(x - 3) + 2 < 5(x - 1)$

3. Factor

   a. $x^2 + 6x + 8$
   b. $x^2 - 5xy - 14y^2$
   c. $z^2 - 9zw - 190w^2$

4. Solve

   a. $x^2 + x - 2 = 0$
   b. $x^2 + x = 12$
   c. $x^2 - 9 = 0$

5. Solve the system of equations:

   a. $2x + y = 4$
      $2x - 3y = 12$
   b. $2x - 3y = 5$
      $x + 3y = 7$

6. Solve
   $$y = x^2 - 3x + 3$$
   $$y = x - 1$$

7. The sum of 15 and twice a certain number is 33. Find that number.

8. Find two numbers whose sum is 18 and whose difference is 4.

Answers

1. a.

$9y + 7 = 4y - 3$	Given
$9y + 7 - 4y = 4y - 3 - 4y$	Subtract $4y$ from both sides.
$5y + 7 = -3$	Combining like terms
$5y + 7 - 7 = -3 - 7$	Subtract 7 from both sides.
$5y = -10$	Combining like terms
$y = \dfrac{-10}{5}$	Multiply both sides by $\dfrac{1}{5}$
$y = -2$	

b.

$3(x + 2) - 1 = x - 2(1 - 3x)$	Given
$3x + 6 - 1 = x - 2 + 6x$	Distributive property
$3x + 5 = -2 + 7x$	Combining like terms
$3x + 5 - 7x = -2 + 7x - 7x$	Subtract $7x$ from both sides.
$-4x + 5 = -2$	Combining like terms
$-4x + 5 - 5 = -2 - 5$	Subtract 5 from both sides.
$-4x = -7$	

$x = \dfrac{-7}{-4}$	Divide both sides by -4.
$x = \dfrac{7}{4}$	

2. a.

$3(y - 2) + 5 > -2y + 4$	Given
$3y - 6 + 5 > -2y + 4$	Distributive property
$3y - 1 > -2y + 4$	Combining like terms
$3y - 1 + 2y > -2y + 4 + 2y$	Add $2y$ to both sides.
$5y - 1 > 4$	Combining like terms
$5y - 1 + 1 > 4 + 1$	Add 1 to both sides.
$5y > 5$	Combining like terms
$y > 1$	Multiply by $\dfrac{1}{5}$, property iii, when $c > 0$.

b.

$4(x - 3) + 2 < 5(x - 1)$	Given
$4x - 12 + 2 < 5x - 5$	Distributive property
$4x - 10 < 5x - 5$	Combining like terms
$4x - 10 - 5x < 5x - 5 - 5x$	Subtract $5x$ from both sides.
$-x - 10 < -5$	Combining like terms
$-x - 10 + 10 < -5 + 10$	Add 10 to both sides.

$-x < 5$ Combining like terms

$x > -5$ Multiply by -1, property iii, when $c < 0$.

3.   a. $x^2 + 6x + 8 = (x + 4)(x + 2)$
     b. $x^2 - 5xy - 14y^2 = (x - 7y)(x + 2y)$
     c. $z^2 - 9zw - 190w^2 = (z - 19w)(z + 10w)$

4.   a. $x^2 + x - 2 = (x + 2)(x - 1) = 0$.
     Therefore, the solution set is $\{-2, 1\}$.
     b. $x^2 + x - 12 = (x + 4)(x - 3) = 0$.
     Therefore, the solution set is $\{-4, 3\}$.
     c. $x^2 - 9 = (x - 3)(x + 3) = 0$. Therefore, the solution set is $\{-3, 3\}$.

5.   a.   Method I:

If the corresponding sides of the second equation, $2x - 3y = 12$, are subtracted from the first equation $2x + y = 4$, the x terms will cancel and an equation with just the variable y will result. So $(2x + y) - (2x - 3y) = 4 - 12$, $2x + y - 2x + 3y = -8$, $4y = -8$, and $y = -2$. Now substitute -2 for y into either original equation and solve for x. The first equation, $2x + y = 4$, will be used here because it appears to be a little easier to work with. Then $2x + (-2) = 4$, $2x - 2 = 4$, $2x = 6$, and $x = 3$. Therefore the solution is $x = 3$ and $y = -2$.

Method II:

Solve the first equation, $2x + y = 4$, for y to get $y = 4 - 2x$. Now substitute $4 - 2x$ for y into the second equation $2x - 3y = 12$, and solve for x. $2x - 3(4 - 2x) = 12$, $2x - 12 + 6x = 12$, $8x = 24$, and $x = 3$.

Now substitute 3 for x into either orginal eqation and solve for y. The first equation, $2x + y = 4$, will be used here because it appears to be a little easier to work with. $2(3) + y = 4$, $6 + y = 4$, and $y = -2$.

b.   Method I:

If the corresponding sides of the two equations are added, the y terms will cancel and an equation with just the variable x will result. $(2x - 3y) + (x + 3y) = 5 + 7$, $2x - 3y + x + 3y = 12$, $3x = 12$, and $x = 4$. Now substitute 4 for x into either original equation and solve for y. The second equation $x + 3y = 7$, will be used here becasue it appears to be a little easier to work with. $4 + 3y = 7$, $3y = 3$, and $y = 1$. Therefore the solution is $x = 4$ and $y = 1$.

Method II:

Solve the second equation, $x + 3y = 7$, for x to get $x = 7 - 3y$. Now substitute $7 - 3y$ for x into the first equation, $2x - 3y = 5$, and solve the resulting for y. $2(7 - 3y) - 3y = 5$, $14 - 6y - 3y = 5$, $-9y = -9$, and $y = 1$. Now substitute 1 for y into either original equation and solve for x. The second equation $x + 3y = 7$, will be used here because it appears to be a little easier to work with. $x + 3(1) = 7$, $x + 3 = 7$, and $x = 4$.

6. Substitute $x - 1$ for y into the equation $y = x^2 - 3x + 3$ and we have $x^2 - 3x + 3 = x - 1$. Solve this equation for x. $x^2 - 4x + 4 = 0$, $(x - 2)^2 = 0$, $x - 2 = 0$, $x = 2$. Substitute $x = 2$ into the first or second equation to get $y = 1$. Therefore, the solution is $(2, 1)$.

7. We need to solve $15 + 2x = 33$. Solving this equation gives us $x = 9$.

8. We need to solve

$$x + y = 18$$
$$x - y = 4$$

If the corresponding sides of the equations are added the y terms will cancel leaving an equation in just the one variable x. $(x + y) + (x - y) = 18 + 4$, $x + y + x - y = 22$, $2x = 22$, $x = 11$. Plug 11 for x into the first equation and solve for y. $11 + y = 18$, and $y = 7$. Therefore the solution is $x = 11$ and $y = 7$.

Chapter 7

Probability and Combinatorics

A. Review of Fundamentals

1. Probability concepts

   Any situation or problem involving uncertain results is called an *experiment*. The various possible results are called *outcomes,* and the set of all possible outcomes is called the *sample space, S,* of the experiment. Any subset of the sample space is called an *event.*

   Example 1:

   The tossing of a coin is an experiment with two possible outcomes, heads or tails. The sample space $S = \{$heads, tails$\}$. There are four possible events:

   1. E = The coin lands heads up, then $E = \{$heads$\}$
   2. A = The coin lands tails up, then $A = \{$tails$\}$
   3. S = The coin lands either heads up or tails up, then $S = \{$heads, tails$\}$
   4. C = the coin lands neither heads up nor tails up, then $C = \varnothing$, the empty set.

   The probability of an event E, denoted by $P(E)$, is the number of outcomes in E divided by the number of outcomes in S. That is,

   $$P(E) = \frac{\text{number of outcomes in } E}{\text{number of outcomes in } S}$$

Example 2:

Consider the experiment of tossing a coin. Let $E =$ The coin lands heads up. Find the probability of E.

Solution:

Since $E = \{$ heads$\}$, $P(E) = \dfrac{1}{2}$

Some properties:

1. $P(\varnothing) = 0$, that is, the probability of an impossible event is zero.
2. $0 \le P(E) \le 1$, for all events E.
3. $P(S) = 1$.
4. $P(A \cup B) = P(A) + P(B) - P(A \cap B)$

Counting Principle: If a first choice can be made in n ways and for each first choice a second choice can be made in m ways, then there are nm possibilities for the pair of choices.

Example 3:

How many two-digit numbers can be made using only the digits 0, 1, and 2?

Solution:

For the first digit we have 3 choices, and for the second digit we have 3 choices. Then we have $3 \times 3 = 9$ different ways of making two-digit numbers by using 0, 1, and 2, as listed:

00	10	20
01	11	21
02	12	22

2. Permutation concepts

An *ordered* arrangement of r elements selected from a set of n elements in such a way that no element can be used more than once is called a *permutation* of n things taken r at a time. The total number of such permutations is denoted by nPr.

Note that $_nPr = \frac{n!}{(n-r)!}$.

Example 1:

If the sample space for an experiment is $\{a, b, c, d\}$, how many permutations of length three can be formed?

Solution:

We are making an arrangement of 3 objects from a set of 4 elements. Then the number of possible arrangements is $\frac{4!}{(4-3)!} = \frac{4!}{1!} = 1 \cdot 2 \cdot 3 \cdot 4 = 24$.

Example 2:

How many ways can the letters of the word CAT be rearranged?

Solution:

The arrangement of 3 objects is to be made from a set of 3 items. Then we have

$_3P_3 = \frac{3!}{(3-3)!} = 3! = 6$ arrangements as listed:

CAT, CTA, ACT, ATC, TCA, and TAC

B. Extension of Work with Permutations

   1. Number of permutations of n objects, r identical, s identical, t identical, etcetera, taken all at a time:

   $$\frac{n!}{r!\,s!\,t!\,\dots}$$

   Example 1:

   How many ways can the letters in the word MISSISSIPPI be arranged?

   Solutions:

   We have $n = 11$ letters, the letter M appears once, I appears 4 times, S appears 4 times, P appears 2 times. Then the total number of arrangements is

   $$\frac{11!}{4!4!2!} = 34{,}650.$$

C. Combinations

   1. Combination of n objects, taken r at a time, $r \le n$

   An *unordered* arrangement of an r element subset of an n element set is called a *combination* of n things taken r at a time. The total number of such combinations is denoted by $_nCr$.

   Note that $_nCr = \dfrac{n!}{(n-r)!\,r!}$.

   Example 1:

   If the sample space for an experiment is $\{a, b, c, d\}$, how many combinations of three letters can be formed?

   Solution:

   We are making a selection of objects from a set of 4 elements. Then the number of possible combinations is $\dfrac{4!}{(4-3)!\,3!} = \dfrac{4!}{1!3!} = \dfrac{1 \cdot 2 \cdot 3 \cdot 4}{3!} = \dfrac{24}{1 \cdot 2 \cdot 3} = 4.$

   Compare this example with example 1 of section B.

2. Distinction between combination and permutation

   In permutations, we are interested in ordered arrangements, that is, order is important. In combinations, the order is not important.

   Example 1:

   Let the sample space for an experiment be $\{a, b, c, d\}$. If we are finding the permutations of length three, $\{a, b, c\}$, $\{a, c, b\}$, $\{b, a, c\}$, $\{b, c, a\}$, $\{c, a, b\}$, and $\{c, b, a\}$ represent 6 different elements, while if we are finding the combinations of length three, they represent the same element.

3. Applications

   Example 1:

   If one card is drawn from an ordinary deck of 52 playing cards, what is the probability that it will be either a club or a face card (king, queen, or jack)?

   Solution:

   Let C = drawing a club, F = drawing a face card. Then $P(C) = \dfrac{13}{52}$, $P(F) = \dfrac{12}{52}$, and $P(C \cap F) = \dfrac{3}{52}$. Therefore,

   $P(C \cup F) = \dfrac{13}{52} + \dfrac{12}{52} - \dfrac{3}{52} = \dfrac{22}{52} = \dfrac{11}{26}$, by property $P(A \cup B) = P(A) + P(B) - P(A \cap B)$.

Questions

1. Rolling a single die is an experiment with six possible outcomes. Its sample space is $S = \{1, 2, 3, 4, 5, 6\}$. Let $E =$ the die falls with an even number facing up. List the elements of E.

2. Consider the experiment of tossing a coin. Let $A =$ The coin lands tails up. Find the probability of A, $P(A)$.

3. Consider the experiment of rolling a die. Let $E = \{$Observe an even number$\}$ and $B = \{$Observe a number less than or equal to 4$\}$. Find $P(E)$ and $P(B)$.

4. How many ways can the letters in the word ARTICHOKE be rearranged?

5. The board of a large corporation has six members willing to be nominated for office. How many different "president; vicepresident; treasurer" slates could be submitted to the stockholders?

6. Calculate and $_4C_2$ and $_8C_2$.

7. A car dealer has three types of cars from which two customers will pick one. How many different sales can the dealer make?

8. A car dealer has two types of cars from which three customers will make a selection. How many different sales can the dealer make?

9. How many groups of five students can be drawn from a total of seven students in which order does not count?

10. The president of the company must select four of her six vice presidents to handle problems when they arise. How many different groups of vice presidents can the president devise?

11. A consumer is asked to rank his preference of five brands of soda. How many different rankings can result?

12. What is the probability that
    a. A thirteen-year-old will be elected president of the United States in the next election?
    b. Somebody will be elected president of the United States in the next election?

13. An urn contains 8 chips, four white, and four blue. Two chips are chosen at random, without replacement. What is the probability that two of them are white?

14. If one card is drawn from a well-shuffled deck of 52 playing cards, what are the probabilities of getting
    a. a red king?
    b. a black card?
    c. a diamond?

Answers

1. $E = \{2, 4, 6\}$

2. Since $A = \{\text{tails}\}$, $P(A) = \frac{1}{2}$.

3. Since $E = 2, 4, 6$, $P(E) = \frac{3}{6} = \frac{1}{2}$, and since

   $B = \{1, 2, 3, 4\}$, $P(B) = \frac{4}{6} = \frac{2}{3}$.

4. The arrangement of 9 objects is to be made from a set of 9 items. Thus we have

   $$_9P_9 = \frac{9!}{(9-9)!} = 9! = 362{,}880 \text{ arrangements}$$

   that can be made.

5. Let's first note that we have 6 elements, and that we are choosing arrangements of three and that the order is important.

   Then $_6P_3 = \dfrac{6!}{(6-3)!} = 6 \cdot 5 \cdot 4 = 120$ differ-

   ent slates could be submitted to the stockholders.

6. $_4C_2 = \dfrac{4!}{2!\,2!} = 6$ and $_8C_2 = \dfrac{8!}{2!\,6!} = 28$.

7. The first customer has three choices, and the second customer has three choices. Therefore, the total number of choices is $3 \cdot 3 = 9$.

8. Each customer has two choices, since there are three customers, the total number of choices is $2 \cdot 2 \cdot 2 = 8$.

9. $_7C_5 = 21$.

10. $_6C_4 = 15$.

11. $5 \cdot 4 \cdot 3 \cdot 2 \cdot 1 = 120$.

12. a. Zero
    b. 1

13. $\dfrac{_4C_2}{_8C_2} = \dfrac{6}{28} = \dfrac{3}{14}$

14. a. $\dfrac{2}{52} = \dfrac{1}{26}$

    b. $\dfrac{26}{52} = \dfrac{1}{2}$

    c. $\dfrac{13}{52} = \dfrac{1}{4}$

Part IV

Practice Tests and Answers

Reference Formulas for Mathematics

Pythagorean and Quotient Identities

$$\sin^2 A + \cos^2 A = 1$$
$$\tan^2 A + 1 = \sec^2 A$$
$$\cot^2 A + 1 = \csc^2 A$$

$$\tan A = \frac{\sin A}{\cos A}$$

$$\cot A = \frac{\cos A}{\sin A}$$

Functions of the Sum of Two Angles

$$\sin (A + B) = \sin A \cos B + \cos A \sin B$$
$$\cos (A + B) = \cos A \cos B - \sin A \sin B$$
$$\tan (A + B) = \frac{\tan A + \tan B}{1 - \tan A \tan B}$$

Functions of the Difference of Two Angles

$$\sin (A - B) = \sin A \cos B - \cos A \sin B$$
$$\cos (A - B) = \cos A \cos B + \sin A \sin B$$
$$\tan (A - B) = \frac{\tan A - \tan B}{1 + \tan A \tan B}$$

Law of Sines

$$\frac{a}{\sin A} = \frac{b}{\sin B} = \frac{c}{\sin C}$$

Law of Cosines

$$a^2 = b^2 + c^2 - 2bc \cos A$$

Functions of the Double Angle

$$\sin 2A = 2 \sin A \cos A$$
$$\cos 2A = \cos^2 A - \sin^2 A$$
$$\cos 2A = 2 \cos^2 A - 1$$
$$\cos 2A = 1 - 2 \sin^2 A$$

$$\tan 2A = \frac{2 \tan A}{1 - \tan^2 A}$$

Functions of the Half Angle

$$\sin \tfrac{1}{2}A = \pm \sqrt{\frac{1 - \cos A}{2}}$$

$$\cos \tfrac{1}{2}A = \pm \sqrt{\frac{1 + \cos A}{2}}$$

$$\tan \tfrac{1}{2}A = \pm \sqrt{\frac{1 - \cos A}{1 + \cos A}}$$

Area of Triangle

$$K = \tfrac{1}{2}ab \sin C$$

Standard Deviation

$$\text{S.D.} = \sqrt{\frac{1}{n} \sum_{i=1}^{n} (\bar{x} - x_i)^2}$$

Table A: Common Logarithms of Numbers*

N	0	1	2	3	4	5	6	7	8	9
10	0000	0043	0086	0128	0170	0212	0253	0294	0334	0374
11	0414	0453	0492	0531	0569	0607	0645	0682	0719	0755
12	0792	0828	0864	0899	0934	0969	1004	1038	1072	1106
13	1139	1173	1206	1239	1271	1303	1335	1367	1399	1430
14	1461	1492	1523	1553	1584	1614	1644	1673	1703	1732
15	1761	1790	1818	1847	1875	1903	1931	1959	1987	2014
16	2041	2068	2095	2122	2148	2175	2201	2227	2253	2279
17	2304	2330	2355	2380	2405	2430	2455	2480	2504	2529
18	2553	2577	2601	2625	2648	2672	2695	2718	2742	2765
19	2788	2810	2833	2856	2878	2900	2923	2945	2967	2989
20	3010	3032	3054	3075	3096	3118	3139	3160	3181	3201
21	3222	3243	3263	3284	3304	3324	3345	3365	3385	3404
22	3424	3444	3464	3483	3502	3522	3541	3560	3579	3598
23	3617	3636	3655	3674	3692	3711	3729	3747	3766	3784
24	3802	3820	3838	3856	3874	3892	3909	3927	3945	3962
25	3979	3997	4014	4031	4048	4065	4082	4099	4116	4133
26	4150	4166	4183	4200	4216	4232	4249	4265	4281	4298
27	4314	4330	4346	4362	4378	4393	4409	4425	4440	4456
28	4472	4487	4502	4518	4533	4548	4564	4579	4594	4609
29	4624	4639	4654	4669	4683	4698	4713	4728	4742	4757
30	4771	4786	4800	4814	4829	4843	4857	4871	4886	4900
31	4914	4928	4942	4955	4969	4983	4997	5011	5024	5038
32	5051	5065	5079	5092	5105	5119	5132	5145	5159	5172
33	5185	5198	5211	5224	5237	5250	5263	5276	5289	5302
34	5315	5328	5340	5353	5366	5378	5391	5403	5416	5428
35	5441	5453	5465	5478	5490	5502	5514	5527	5539	5551
36	5563	5575	5587	5599	5611	5623	5635	5647	5658	5670
37	5682	5694	5705	5717	5729	5740	5752	5763	5775	5786
38	5798	5809	5821	5832	5843	5855	5866	5877	5888	5899
39	5911	5922	5933	5944	5955	5966	5977	5988	5999	6010
40	6021	6031	6042	6053	6064	6075	6085	6096	6107	6117
41	6128	6138	6149	6160	6170	6180	6191	6201	6212	6222
42	6232	6243	6253	6263	6274	6284	6294	6304	6314	6325
43	6335	6345	6355	6365	6375	6385	6395	6405	6415	6425
44	6435	6444	6454	6464	6474	6484	6493	6503	6513	6522
45	6532	6542	6551	6561	6571	6580	6590	6599	6609	6618
46	6628	6637	6646	6656	6665	6675	6684	6693	6702	6712
47	6721	6730	6739	6749	6758	6767	6776	6785	6794	6803
48	6812	6821	6830	6839	6848	6857	6866	6875	6884	6893
49	6902	6911	6920	6928	6937	6946	6955	6964	6972	6981
50	6990	6998	7007	7016	7024	7033	7042	7050	7059	7067
51	7076	7084	7093	7101	7110	7118	7126	7135	7143	7152
52	7160	7168	7177	7185	7193	7202	7210	7218	7226	7235
53	7243	7251	7259	7267	7275	7284	7292	7300	7308	7316
54	7324	7332	7340	7348	7356	7364	7372	7380	7388	7396
N	0	1	2	3	4	5	6	7	8	9

* This table gives the mantissas of numbers with the decimal point omitted in each case. Characteristics are determined from the numbers by inspection.

Table A: Common Logarithms of Numbers*

N	0	1	2	3	4	5	6	7	8	9
55	7404	7412	7419	7427	7435	7443	7451	7459	7466	7474
56	7482	7490	7497	7505	7513	7520	7528	7536	7543	7551
57	7559	7566	7574	7582	7589	7597	7604	7612	7619	7627
58	7634	7642	7649	7657	7664	7672	7679	7686	7694	7701
59	7709	7716	7723	7731	7738	7745	7752	7760	7767	7774
60	7782	7789	7796	7803	7810	7818	7825	7832	7839	7846
61	7853	7860	7868	7875	7882	7889	7896	7903	7910	7917
62	7924	7931	7938	7945	7952	7959	7966	7973	7980	7987
63	7993	8000	8007	8014	8021	8028	8035	8041	8048	8055
64	8062	8069	8075	8082	8089	8096	8102	8109	8116	8122
65	8129	8136	8142	8149	8156	8162	8169	8176	8182	8189
66	8195	8202	8209	8215	8222	8228	8235	8241	8248	8254
67	8261	8267	8274	8280	8287	8293	8299	8306	8312	8319
68	8325	8331	8338	8344	8351	8357	8363	8370	8376	8382
69	8388	8395	8401	8407	8414	8420	8426	8432	8439	8445
70	8451	8457	8463	8470	8476	8482	8488	8494	8500	8506
71	8513	8519	8525	8531	8537	8543	8549	8555	8561	8567
72	8573	8579	8585	8591	8597	8603	8609	8615	8621	8627
73	8633	8639	8645	8651	8657	8663	8669	8675	8681	8686
74	8692	8698	8704	8710	8716	8722	8727	8733	8739	8745
75	8751	8756	8762	8768	8774	8779	8785	8791	8797	8802
76	8808	8814	8820	8825	8831	8837	8842	8848	8854	8859
77	8865	8871	8876	8882	8887	8893	8899	8904	8910	8915
78	8921	8927	8932	8938	8943	8949	8954	8960	8965	8971
79	8976	8982	8987	8993	8998	9004	9009	9015	9020	9025
80	9031	9036	9042	9047	9053	9058	9063	9069	9074	9079
81	9085	9090	9096	9101	9106	9112	9117	9122	9128	9133
82	9138	9143	9149	9154	9159	9165	9170	9175	9180	9186
83	9191	9196	9201	9206	9212	9217	9222	9227	9232	9238
84	9243	9248	9253	9258	9263	9269	9274	9279	9284	9289
85	9294	9299	9304	9309	9315	9320	9325	9330	9335	9340
86	9345	9350	9355	9360	9365	9370	9375	9380	9385	9390
87	9395	9400	9405	9410	9415	9420	9425	9430	9435	9440
88	9445	9450	9455	9460	9465	9469	9474	9479	9484	9489
89	9494	9499	9504	9509	9513	9518	9523	9528	9533	9538
90	9542	9547	9552	9557	9562	9566	9571	9576	9581	9586
91	9590	9595	9600	9605	9609	9614	9619	9624	9628	9633
92	9638	9643	9647	9652	9657	9661	9666	9671	9675	9680
93	9685	9689	9694	9699	9703	9708	9713	9717	9722	9727
94	9731	9736	9741	9745	9750	9754	9759	9763	9768	9773
95	9777	9782	9786	9791	9795	9800	9805	9809	9814	9818
96	9823	9827	9832	9836	9841	9845	9850	9854	9859	9863
97	9868	9872	9877	9881	9886	9890	9894	9899	9903	9908
98	9912	9917	9921	9926	9930	9934	9939	9943	9948	9952
99	9956	9961	9965	9969	9974	9978	9983	9987	9991	9996
N	0	1	2	3	4	5	6	7	8	9

* This table gives the mantissas of numbers with the decimal point omitted in each case. Characteristics are determined from the numbers by inspection.

Table B: Values of Trigonometric Functions

Angle	Sin	Cos	Tan	Cot	
0° 00′	.0000	1.0000	.0000	—	90° 00′
10	.0029	1.0000	.0029	343.77	50
20	.0058	1.0000	.0058	171.89	40
30	.0087	1.0000	.0087	114.59	30
40	.0116	.9999	.0116	85.940	20
50	.0145	.9999	.0145	68.750	10
1° 00′	.0175	.9998	.0175	57.290	89° 00′
10	.0204	.9998	.0204	49.104	50
20	.0233	.9997	.0233	42.964	40
30	.0262	.9997	.0262	38.188	30
40	.0291	.9996	.0291	34.368	20
50	.0320	.9995	.0320	31.242	10
2° 00′	.0349	.9994	.0349	28.636	88° 00′
10	.0378	.9993	.0378	26.432	50
20	.0407	.9992	.0407	24.542	40
30	.0436	.9990	.0437	22.904	30
40	.0465	.9989	.0466	21.470	20
50	.0494	.9988	.0495	20.206	10
3° 00′	.0523	.9986	.0524	19.081	87° 00′
10	.0552	.9985	.0553	18.075	50
20	.0581	.9983	.0582	17.169	40
30	.0610	.9981	.0612	16.350	30
40	.0640	.9980	.0641	15.605	20
50	.0669	.9978	.0670	14.924	10
4° 00′	.0698	.9976	.0699	14.301	86° 00′
10	.0727	.9974	.0729	13.727	50
20	.0756	.9971	.0758	13.197	40
30	.0785	.9969	.0787	12.706	30
40	.0814	.9967	.0816	12.251	20
50	.0843	.9964	.0846	11.826	10
5° 00′	.0872	.9962	.0875	11.430	85° 00′
10	.0901	.9959	.0904	11.059	50
20	.0929	.9957	.0934	10.712	40
30	.0958	.9954	.0963	10.385	30
40	.0987	.9951	.0992	10.078	20
50	.1016	.9948	.1022	9.7882	10
6° 00′	.1045	.9945	.1051	9.5144	84° 00′
10	.1074	.9942	.1080	9.2553	50
20	.1103	.9939	.1110	9.0098	40
30	.1132	.9936	.1139	8.7769	30
40	.1161	.9932	.1169	8.5555	20
50	.1190	.9929	.1198	8.3450	10
7° 00′	.1219	.9925	.1228	8.1443	83° 00′
10	.1248	.9922	.1257	7.9530	50
20	.1276	.9918	.1287	7.7704	40
30	.1305	.9914	.1317	7.5958	30
40	.1334	.9911	.1346	7.4287	20
50	.1363	.9907	.1376	7.2687	10
8° 00′	.1392	.9903	.1405	7.1154	82° 00′
10	.1421	.9899	.1435	6.9682	50
20	.1449	.9894	.1465	6.8269	40
30	.1478	.9890	.1495	6.6912	30
40	.1507	.9886	.1524	6.5606	20
50	.1536	.9881	.1554	6.4348	10
9° 00′	.1564	.9877	.1584	6.3138	81° 00′
10	.1593	.9872	.1614	6.1970	50
20	.1622	.9868	.1644	6.0844	40
30	.1650	.9863	.1673	5.9758	30
40	.1679	.9858	.1703	5.8708	20
50	.1708	.9853	.1733	5.7694	10
10° 00′	.1736	.9848	.1763	5.6713	80° 00′
10	.1765	.9843	.1793	5.5764	50
20	.1794	.9838	.1823	5.4845	40
30	.1822	.9833	.1853	5.3955	30
40	.1851	.9827	.1883	5.3093	20
50	.1880	.9822	.1914	5.2257	10
11° 00′	.1908	.9816	.1944	5.1446	79° 00′
10	.1937	.9811	.1974	5.0658	50
20	.1965	.9805	.2004	4.9894	40
30	.1994	.9799	.2035	4.9152	30
40	.2022	.9793	.2065	4.8430	20
50	.2051	.9787	.2095	4.7729	10
12° 00′	.2079	.9781	.2126	4.7046	78° 00′
	Cos	Sin	Cot	Tan	Angle

Angle	Sin	Cos	Tan	Cot	
12° 00′	.2079	.9781	.2126	4.7046	78° 00′
10	.2108	.9775	.2156	4.6382	50
20	.2136	.9769	.2186	4.5736	40
30	.2164	.9763	.2217	4.5107	30
40	.2193	.9757	.2247	4.4494	20
50	.2221	.9750	.2278	4.3897	10
13° 00′	.2250	.9744	.2309	4.3315	77° 00′
10	.2278	.9737	.2339	4.2747	50
20	.2306	.9730	.2370	4.2193	40
30	.2334	.9724	.2401	4.1653	30
40	.2363	.9717	.2432	4.1126	20
50	.2391	.9710	.2462	4.0611	10
14° 00′	.2419	.9703	.2493	4.0108	76° 00′
10	.2447	.9696	.2524	3.9617	50
20	.2476	.9689	.2555	3.9136	40
30	.2504	.9681	.2586	3.8667	30
40	.2532	.9674	.2617	3.8208	20
50	.2560	.9667	.2648	3.7760	10
15° 00′	.2588	.9659	.2679	3.7321	75° 00′
10	.2616	.9652	.2711	3.6891	50
20	.2644	.9644	.2742	3.6470	40
30	.2672	.9636	.2773	3.6059	30
40	.2700	.9628	.2805	3.5656	20
50	.2728	.9621	.2836	3.5261	10
16° 00′	.2756	.9613	.2867	3.4874	74° 00′
10	.2784	.9605	.2899	3.4495	50
20	.2812	.9596	.2931	3.4124	40
30	.2840	.9588	.2962	3.3759	30
40	.2868	.9580	.2994	3.3402	20
50	.2896	.9572	.3026	3.3052	10
17° 00′	.2924	.9563	.3057	3.2709	73° 00′
10	.2952	.9555	.3089	3.2371	50
20	.2979	.9546	.3121	3.2041	40
30	.3007	.9537	.3153	3.1716	30
40	.3035	.9528	.3185	3.1397	20
50	.3062	.9520	.3217	3.1084	10
18° 00′	.3090	.9511	.3249	3.0777	72° 00′
10	.3118	.9502	.3281	3.0475	50
20	.3145	.9492	.3314	3.0178	40
30	.3173	.9483	.3346	2.9887	30
40	.3201	.9474	.3378	2.9600	20
50	.3228	.9465	.3411	2.9319	10
19° 00′	.3256	.9455	.3443	2.9042	71° 00′
10	.3283	.9446	.3476	2.8770	50
20	.3311	.9436	.3508	2.8502	40
30	.3338	.9426	.3541	2.8239	30
40	.3365	.9417	.3574	2.7980	20
50	.3393	.9407	.3607	2.7725	10
20° 00′	.3420	.9397	.3640	2.7475	70° 00′
10	.3448	.9387	.3673	2.7228	50
20	.3475	.9377	.3706	2.6985	40
30	.3502	.9367	.3739	2.6746	30
40	.3529	.9356	.3772	2.6511	20
50	.3557	.9346	.3805	2.6279	10
21° 00′	.3584	.9336	.3839	2.6051	69° 00′
10	.3611	.9325	.3872	2.5826	50
20	.3638	.9315	.3906	2.5605	40
30	.3665	.9304	.3939	2.5386	30
40	.3692	.9293	.3973	2.5172	20
50	.3719	.9283	.4006	2.4960	10
22° 00′	.3746	.9272	.4040	2.4751	68° 00′
10	.3773	.9261	.4074	2.4545	50
20	.3800	.9250	.4108	2.4342	40
30	.3827	.9239	.4142	2.4142	30
40	.3854	.9228	.4176	2.3945	20
50	.3881	.9216	.4210	2.3750	10
23° 00′	.3907	.9205	.4245	2.3559	67° 00′
10	.3934	.9194	.4279	2.3369	50
20	.3961	.9182	.4314	2.3183	40
30	.3987	.9171	.4348	2.2998	30
40	.4014	.9159	.4383	2.2817	20
50	.4041	.9147	.4417	2.2637	10
24° 00′	.4067	.9135	.4452	2.2460	66° 00′
	Cos	Sin	Cot	Tan	Angle

Table B: Values of Trigonometric Functions

Angle		Sin	Cos	Tan	Cot		
24°	00'	.4067	.9135	.4452	2.2460	66°	00'
	10	.4094	.9124	.4487	2.2286		50
	20	.4120	.9112	.4522	2.2113		40
	30	.4147	.9100	.4557	2.1943		30
	40	.4173	.9088	.4592	2.1775		20
	50	.4200	.9075	.4628	2.1609		10
25°	00'	.4226	.9063	.4663	2.1445	65°	00'
	10	.4253	.9051	.4699	2.1283		50
	20	.4279	.9038	.4734	2.1123		40
	30	.4305	.9026	.4770	2.0965		30
	40	.4331	.9013	.4806	2.0809		20
	50	.4358	.9001	.4841	2.0655		10
26°	00'	.4384	.8988	.4877	2.0503	64°	00'
	10	.4410	.8975	.4913	2.0353		50
	20	.4436	.8962	.4950	2.0204		40
	30	.4462	.8949	.4986	2.0057		30
	40	.4488	.8936	.5022	1.9912		20
	50	.4514	.8923	.5059	1.9768		10
27°	00'	.4540	.8910	.5095	1.9626	63°	00'
	10	.4566	.8897	.5132	1.9486		50
	20	.4592	.8884	.5169	1.9347		40
	30	.4617	.8870	.5206	1.9210		30
	40	.4643	.8857	.5243	1.9074		20
	50	.4669	.8843	.5280	1.8940		10
28°	00'	.4695	.8829	.5317	1.8807	62°	00'
	10	.4720	.8816	.5354	1.8676		50
	20	.4746	.8802	.5392	1.8546		40
	30	.4772	.8788	.5430	1.8418		30
	40	.4797	.8774	.5467	1.8291		20
	50	.4823	.8760	.5505	1.8165		10
29°	00'	.4848	.8746	.5543	1.8040	61°	00'
	10	.4874	.8732	.5581	1.7917		50
	20	.4899	.8718	.5619	1.7796		40
	30	.4924	.8704	.5658	1.7675		30
	40	.4950	.8689	.5696	1.7556		20
	50	.4975	.8675	.5735	1.7437		10
30°	00'	.5000	.8660	.5774	1.7321	60°	00'
	10	.5025	.8646	.5812	1.7205		50
	20	.5050	.8631	.5851	1.7090		40
	30	.5075	.8616	.5890	1.6977		30
	40	.5100	.8601	.5930	1.6864		20
	50	.5125	.8587	.5969	1.6753		10
31°	00'	.5150	.8572	.6009	1.6643	59°	00'
	10	.5175	.8557	.6048	1.6534		50
	20	.5200	.8542	.6088	1.6426		40
	30	.5225	.8526	.6128	1.6319		30
	40	.5250	.8511	.6168	1.6212		20
	50	.5275	.8496	.6208	1.6107		10
32°	00'	.5299	.8480	.6249	1.6003	58°	00'
	10	.5324	.8465	.6289	1.5900		50
	20	.5348	.8450	.6330	1.5798		40
	30	.5373	.8434	.6371	1.5697		30
	40	.5398	.8418	.6412	1.5597		20
	50	.5422	.8403	.6453	1.5497		10
33°	00'	.5446	.8387	.6494	1.5399	57°	00'
	10	.5471	.8371	.6536	1.5301		50
	20	.5495	.8355	.6577	1.5204		40
	30	.5519	.8339	.6619	1.5108		30
	40	.5544	.8323	.6661	1.5013		20
	50	.5568	.8307	.6703	1.4919		10
34°	00'	.5592	.8290	.6745	1.4826	56°	00'
	10	.5616	.8274	.6787	1.4733		50
	20	.5640	.8258	.6830	1.4641		40
	30	.5664	.8241	.6873	1.4550		30
	40	.5688	.8225	.6916	1.4460		20
	50	.5712	.8208	.6959	1.4370		10
35°	00'	.5736	.8192	.7002	1.4281	55°	00'
	10	.5760	.8175	.7046	1.4193		50
	20	.5783	.8158	.7089	1.4106		40
	30	.5807	.8141	.7133	1.4019		30
	40	.5831	.8124	.7177	1.3934		20
	50	.5854	.8107	.7221	1.3848		10
36°	00'	.5878	.8090	.7265	1.3764	54°	00'
		Cos	Sin	Cot	Tan	Angle	

Angle		Sin	Cos	Tan	Cot		
36°	00'	.5878	.8090	.7265	1.3764	54°	00'
	10	.5901	.8073	.7310	1.3680		50
	20	.5925	.8056	.7355	1.3597		40
	30	.5948	.8039	.7400	1.3514		30
	40	.5972	.8021	.7445	1.3432		20
	50	.5995	.8004	.7490	1.3351		10
37°	00'	.6018	.7986	.7536	1.3270	53°	00'
	10	.6041	.7969	.7581	1.3190		50
	20	.6065	.7951	.7627	1.3111		40
	30	.6088	.7934	.7673	1.3032		30
	40	.6111	.7916	.7720	1.2954		20
	50	.6134	.7898	.7766	1.2876		10
38°	00'	.6157	.7880	.7813	1.2799	52°	00'
	10	.6180	.7862	.7860	1.2723		50
	20	.6202	.7844	.7907	1.2647		40
	30	.6225	.7826	.7954	1.2572		30
	40	.6248	.7808	.8002	1.2497		20
	50	.6271	.7790	.8050	1.2423		10
39°	00'	.6293	.7771	.8098	1.2349	51°	00'
	10	.6316	.7753	.8146	1.2276		50
	20	.6338	.7735	.8195	1.2203		40
	30	.6361	.7716	.8243	1.2131		30
	40	.6383	.7698	.8292	1.2059		20
	50	.6406	.7679	.8342	1.1988		10
40°	00'	.6428	.7660	.8391	1.1918	50°	00'
	10	.6450	.7642	.8441	1.1847		50
	20	.6472	.7623	.8491	1.1778		40
	30	.6494	.7604	.8541	1.1708		30
	40	.6517	.7585	.8591	1.1640		20
	50	.6539	.7566	.8642	1.1571		10
41°	00'	.6561	.7547	.8693	1.1504	49°	00'
	10	.6583	.7528	.8744	1.1436		50
	20	.6604	.7509	.8796	1.1369		40
	30	.6626	.7490	.8847	1.1303		30
	40	.6648	.7470	.8899	1.1237		20
	50	.6670	.7451	.8952	1.1171		10
42°	00'	.6691	.7431	.9004	1.1106	48°	00'
	10	.6713	.7412	.9057	1.1041		50
	20	.6734	.7392	.9110	1.0977		40
	30	.6756	.7373	.9163	1.0913		30
	40	.6777	.7353	.9217	1.0850		20
	50	.6799	.7333	.9271	1.0786		10
43°	00'	.6820	.7314	.9325	1.0724	47°	00'
	10	.6841	.7294	.9380	1.0661		50
	20	.6862	.7274	.9435	1.0599		40
	30	.6884	.7254	.9490	1.0538		30
	40	.6905	.7234	.9545	1.0477		20
	50	.6926	.7214	.9601	1.0416		10
44°	00'	.6947	.7193	.9657	1.0355	46°	00'
	10	.6967	.7173	.9713	1.0295		50
	20	.6988	.7153	.9770	1.0235		40
	30	.7009	.7133	.9827	1.0176		30
	40	.7030	.7112	.9884	1.0117		20
	50	.7050	.7092	.9942	1.0058		10
45°	00'	.7071	.7071	1.0000	1.0000	45°	00'
		Cos	Sin	Cot	Tan	Angle	

Table C: Logarithms of Trigonometric Functions*

Angle	L Sin	L Cos	L Tan	L Cot	
0° 00′	—	10.0000	—	—	90° 00′
10	7.4637	10.0000	7.4637	12.5363	50
20	7.7648	10.0000	7.7648	12.2352	40
30	7.9408	10.0000	7.9409	12.0591	30
40	8.0658	10.0000	8.0658	11.9342	20
50	8.1627	10.0000	8.1627	11.8373	10
1° 00′	8.2419	9.9999	8.2419	11.7581	89° 00′
10	8.3088	9.9999	8.3089	11.6911	50
20	8.3668	9.9999	8.3669	11.6331	40
30	8.4179	9.9999	8.4181	11.5819	30
40	8.4637	9.9998	8.4638	11.5362	20
50	8.5053	9.9998	8.5053	11.4947	10
2° 00′	8.5428	9.9997	8.5431	11.4569	88° 00′
10	8.5776	9.9997	8.5779	11.4221	50
20	8.6097	9.9996	8.6101	11.3899	40
30	8.6397	9.9996	8.6401	11.3599	30
40	8.6677	9.9995	8.6682	11.3318	20
50	8.6940	9.9995	8.6945	11.3055	10
3° 00′	8.7188	9.9994	8.7194	11.2806	87° 00′
10	8.7423	9.9993	8.7429	11.2571	50
20	8.7645	9.9993	8.7652	11.2348	40
30	8.7857	9.9992	8.7865	11.2135	30
40	8.8059	9.9991	8.8067	11.1933	20
50	8.8251	9.9990	8.8261	11.1739	10
4° 00′	8.8436	9.9989	8.8446	11.1554	86° 00′
10	8.8613	9.9989	8.8624	11.1376	50
20	8.8783	9.9988	8.8795	11.1205	40
30	8.8946	9.9987	8.8960	11.1040	30
40	8.9104	9.9986	8.9118	11.0882	20
50	8.9256	9.9985	8.9272	11.0728	10
5° 00′	8.9403	9.9983	8.9420	11.0580	85° 00′
10	8.9545	9.9982	8.9563	11.0437	50
20	8.9682	9.9981	8.9701	11.0299	40
30	8.9816	9.9980	8.9836	11.0164	30
40	8.9945	9.9979	8.9966	11.0034	20
50	9.0070	9.9977	9.0093	10.9907	10
6° 00′	9.0192	9.9976	9.0216	10.9784	84° 00′
10	9.0311	9.9975	9.0336	10.9664	50
20	9.0426	9.9973	9.0453	10.9547	40
30	9.0539	9.9972	9.0567	10.9433	30
40	9.0648	9.9971	9.0678	10.9322	20
50	9.0755	9.9969	9.0786	10.9214	10
7° 00′	9.0859	9.9968	9.0891	10.9109	83° 00′
10	9.0961	9.9966	9.0995	10.9005	50
20	9.1060	9.9964	9.1096	10.8904	40
30	9.1157	9.9963	9.1194	10.8806	30
40	9.1252	9.9961	9.1291	10.8709	20
50	9.1345	9.9959	9.1385	10.8615	10
8° 00′	9.1436	9.9958	9.1478	10.8522	82° 00′
10	9.1525	9.9956	9.1569	10.8431	50
20	9.1612	9.9954	9.1658	10.8342	40
30	9.1697	9.9952	9.1745	10.8255	30
40	9.1781	9.9950	9.1831	10.8169	20
50	9.1863	9.9948	9.1915	10.8085	10
9° 00′	9.1943	9.9946	9.1997	10.8003	81° 00′
10	9.2022	9.9944	9.2078	10.7922	50
20	9.2100	9.9942	9.2158	10.7842	40
30	9.2176	9.9940	9.2236	10.7764	30
40	9.2251	9.9938	9.2313	10.7687	20
50	9.2324	9.9936	9.2389	10.7611	10
10° 00′	9.2397	9.9934	9.2463	10.7537	80° 00′
10	9.2468	9.9931	9.2536	10.7464	50
20	9.2538	9.9929	9.2609	10.7391	40
30	9.2606	9.9927	9.2680	10.7320	30
40	9.2674	9.9924	9.2750	10.7250	20
50	9.2740	9.9922	9.2819	10.7181	10
11° 00′	9.2806	9.9919	9.2887	10.7113	79° 00′
10	9.2870	9.9917	9.2953	10.7047	50
20	9.2934	9.9914	9.3020	10.6980	40
30	9.2997	9.9912	9.3085	10.6915	30
40	9.3058	9.9909	9.3149	10.6851	20
50	9.3119	9.9907	9.3212	10.6788	10
12° 00′	9.3179	9.9904	9.3275	10.6725	78° 00′
	L Cos	L Sin	L Cot	L Tan	Angle

Angle	L Sin	L Cos	L Tan	L Cot	
12° 00′	9.3179	9.9904	9.3275	10.6725	78° 00′
10	9.3238	9.9901	9.3336	10.6664	50
20	9.3296	9.9899	9.3397	10.6603	40
30	9.3353	9.9896	9.3458	10.6542	30
40	9.3410	9.9893	9.3517	10.6483	20
50	9.3466	9.9890	9.3576	10.6424	10
13° 00′	9.3521	9.9887	9.3634	10.6366	77° 00′
10	9.3575	9.9884	9.3691	10.6309	50
20	9.3629	9.9881	9.3748	10.6252	40
30	9.3682	9.9878	9.3804	10.6196	30
40	9.3734	9.9875	9.3859	10.6141	20
50	9.3786	9.9872	9.3914	10.6086	10
14° 00′	9.3837	9.9869	9.3968	10.6032	76° 00′
10	9.3887	9.9866	9.4021	10.5979	50
20	9.3937	9.9863	9.4074	10.5926	40
30	9.3986	9.9859	9.4127	10.5873	30
40	9.4035	9.9856	9.4178	10.5822	20
50	9.4083	9.9853	9.4230	10.5770	10
15° 00′	9.4130	9.9849	9.4281	10.5719	75° 00′
10	9.4177	9.9846	9.4331	10.5669	50
20	9.4223	9.9843	9.4381	10.5619	40
30	9.4269	9.9839	9.4430	10.5570	30
40	9.4314	9.9836	9.4479	10.5521	20
50	9.4359	9.9832	9.4527	10.5473	10
16° 00′	9.4403	9.9828	9.4575	10.5425	74° 00′
10	9.4447	9.9825	9.4622	10.5378	50
20	9.4491	9.9821	9.4669	10.5331	40
30	9.4533	9.9817	9.4716	10.5284	30
40	9.4576	9.9814	9.4762	10.5238	20
50	9.4618	9.9810	9.4808	10.5192	10
17° 00′	9.4659	9.9806	9.4853	10.5147	73° 00′
10	9.4700	9.9802	9.4898	10.5102	50
20	9.4741	9.9798	9.4943	10.5057	40
30	9.4781	9.9794	9.4987	10.5013	30
40	9.4821	9.9790	9.5031	10.4969	20
50	9.4861	9.9786	9.5075	10.4925	10
18° 00′	9.4900	9.9782	9.5118	10.4882	72° 00′
10	9.4939	9.9778	9.5161	10.4839	50
20	9.4977	9.9774	9.5203	10.4797	40
30	9.5015	9.9770	9.5245	10.4755	30
40	9.5052	9.9765	9.5287	10.4713	20
50	9.5090	9.9761	9.5329	10.4671	10
19° 00′	9.5126	9.9757	9.5370	10.4630	71° 00′
10	9.5163	9.9752	9.5411	10.4589	50
20	9.5199	9.9748	9.5451	10.4549	40
30	9.5235	9.9743	9.5491	10.4509	30
40	9.5270	9.9739	9.5531	10.4469	20
50	9.5306	9.9734	9.5571	10.4429	10
20° 00′	9.5341	9.9730	9.5611	10.4389	70° 00′
10	9.5375	9.9725	9.5650	10.4350	50
20	9.5409	9.9721	9.5689	10.4311	40
30	9.5443	9.9716	9.5727	10.4273	30
40	9.5477	9.9711	9.5766	10.4234	20
50	9.5510	9.9706	9.5804	10.4196	10
21° 00′	9.5543	9.9702	9.5842	10.4158	69° 00′
10	9.5576	9.9697	9.5879	10.4121	50
20	9.5609	9.9692	9.5917	10.4083	40
30	9.5641	9.9687	9.5954	10.4046	30
40	9.5673	9.9682	9.5991	10.4009	20
50	9.5704	9.9677	9.6028	10.3972	10
22° 00′	9.5736	9.9672	9.6064	10.3936	68° 00′
10	9.5767	9.9667	9.6100	10.3900	50
20	9.5798	9.9661	9.6136	10.3864	40
30	9.5828	9.9656	9.6172	10.3828	30
40	9.5859	9.9651	9.6208	10.3792	20
50	9.5889	9.9646	9.6243	10.3757	10
23° 00′	9.5919	9.9640	9.6279	10.3721	67° 00′
10	9.5948	9.9635	9.6314	10.3686	50
20	9.5978	9.9629	9.6348	10.3652	40
30	9.6007	9.9624	9.6383	10.3617	30
40	9.6036	9.9618	9.6417	10.3583	20
50	9.6065	9.9613	9.6452	10.3548	10
24° 00′	9.6093	9.9607	9.6486	10.3514	66° 00′
	L Cos	L Sin	L Cot	L Tan	Angle

* These tables give the logarithms increased by 10. Hence in each case 10 should be subtracted.

Table C: Logarithms of Trigonometric Functions*

Angle	L Sin	L Cos	L Tan	L Cot	
24° 00'	9.6093	9.9607	9.6486	10.3514	66° 00'
10	9.6121	9.9602	9.6520	10.3480	50
20	9.6149	9.9596	9.6553	10.3447	40
30	9.6177	9.9590	9.6587	10.3413	30
40	9.6205	9.9584	9.6620	10.3380	20
50	9.6232	9.9579	9.6654	10.3346	10
25° 00'	9.6259	9.9573	9.6687	10.3313	65° 00'
10	9.6286	9.9567	9.6720	10.3280	50
20	9.6313	9.9561	9.6752	10.3248	40
30	9.6340	9.9555	9.6785	10.3215	30
40	9.6366	9.9549	9.6817	10.3183	20
50	9.6392	9.9543	9.6850	10.3150	10
26° 00'	9.6418	9.9537	9.6882	10.3118	64° 00'
10	9.6444	9.9530	9.6914	10.3086	50
20	9.6470	9.9524	9.6946	10.3054	40
30	9.6495	9.9518	9.6977	10.3023	30
40	9.6521	9.9512	9.7009	10.2991	20
50	9.6546	9.9505	9.7040	10.2960	10
27° 00'	9.6570	9.9499	9.7072	10.2928	63° 00'
10	9.6595	9.9492	9.7103	10.2897	50
20	9.6620	9.9486	9.7134	10.2866	40
30	9.6644	9.9479	9.7165	10.2835	30
40	9.6668	9.9473	9.7196	10.2804	20
50	9.6692	9.9466	9.7226	10.2774	10
28° 00'	9.6716	9.9459	9.7257	10.2743	62° 00'
10	9.6740	9.9453	9.7287	10.2713	50
20	9.6763	9.9446	9.7317	10.2683	40
30	9.6787	9.9439	9.7348	10.2652	30
40	9.6810	9.9432	9.7378	10.2622	20
50	9.6833	9.9425	9.7408	10.2592	10
29° 00'	9.6856	9.9418	9.7438	10.2562	61° 00'
10	9.6878	9.9411	9.7467	10.2533	50
20	9.6901	9.9404	9.7497	10.2503	40
30	9.6923	9.9397	9.7526	10.2474	30
40	9.6946	9.9390	9.7556	10.2444	20
50	9.6968	9.9383	9.7585	10.2415	10
30° 00'	9.6990	9.9375	9.7614	10.2386	60° 00'
10	9.7012	9.9368	9.7644	10.2356	50
20	9.7033	9.9361	9.7673	10.2327	40
30	9.7055	9.9353	9.7701	10.2299	30
40	9.7076	9.9346	9.7730	10.2270	20
50	9.7097	9.9338	9.7759	10.2241	10
31° 00'	9.7118	9.9331	9.7788	10.2212	59° 00'
10	9.7139	9.9323	9.7816	10.2184	50
20	9.7160	9.9315	9.7845	10.2155	40
30	9.7181	9.9308	9.7873	10.2127	30
40	9.7201	9.9300	9.7902	10.2098	20
50	9.7222	9.9292	9.7930	10.2070	10
32° 00'	9.7242	9.9284	9.7958	10.2042	58° 00'
10	9.7262	9.9276	9.7986	10.2014	50
20	9.7282	9.9268	9.8014	10.1986	40
30	9.7302	9.9260	9.8042	10.1958	30
40	9.7322	9.9252	9.8070	10.1930	20
50	9.7342	9.9244	9.8097	10.1903	10
33° 00'	9.7361	9.9236	9.8125	10.1875	57° 00'
10	9.7380	9.9228	9.8153	10.1847	50
20	9.7400	9.9219	9.8180	10.1820	40
30	9.7419	9.9211	9.8208	10.1792	30
40	9.7438	9.9203	9.8235	10.1765	20
50	9.7457	9.9194	9.8263	10.1737	10
34° 00'	9.7476	9.9186	9.8290	10.1710	56° 00'
10	9.7494	9.9177	9.8317	10.1683	50
20	9.7513	9.9169	9.8344	10.1656	40
30	9.7531	9.9160	9.8371	10.1629	30
40	9.7550	9.9151	9.8398	10.1602	20
50	9.7568	9.9142	9.8425	10.1575	10
35° 00'	9.7586	9.9134	9.8452	10.1548	55° 00'
10	9.7604	9.9125	9.8479	10.1521	50
20	9.7622	9.9116	9.8506	10.1494	40
30	9.7640	9.9107	9.8533	10.1467	30
40	9.7657	9.9098	9.8559	10.1441	20
50	9.7675	9.9089	9.8586	10.1414	10
36° 00'	9.7692	9.9080	9.8613	10.1387	54° 00'
	L Cos	L Sin	L Cot	L Tan	Angle

Angle	L Sin	L Cos	L Tan	L Cot	
36° 00'	9.7692	9.9080	9.8613	10.1387	54° 00'
10	9.7710	9.9070	9.8639	10.1361	50
20	9.7727	9.9061	9.8666	10.1334	40
30	9.7744	9.9052	9.8692	10.1308	30
40	9.7761	9.9042	9.8718	10.1282	20
50	9.7778	9.9033	9.8745	10.1255	10
37° 00'	9.7795	9.9023	9.8771	10.1229	53° 00'
10	9.7811	9.9014	9.8797	10.1203	50
20	9.7828	9.9004	9.8824	10.1176	40
30	9.7844	9.8995	9.8850	10.1150	30
40	9.7861	9.8985	9.8876	10.1124	20
50	9.7877	9.8975	9.8902	10.1098	10
38° 00'	9.7893	9.8965	9.8928	10.1072	52° 00'
10	9.7910	9.8955	9.8954	10.1046	50
20	9.7926	9.8945	9.8980	10.1020	40
30	9.7941	9.8935	9.9006	10.0994	30
40	9.7957	9.8925	9.9032	10.0968	20
50	9.7973	9.8915	9.9058	10.0942	10
39° 00'	9.7989	9.8905	9.9084	10.0916	51° 00'
10	9.8004	9.8895	9.9110	10.0890	50
20	9.8020	9.8884	9.9135	10.0865	40
30	9.8035	9.8874	9.9161	10.0839	30
40	9.8050	9.8864	9.9187	10.0813	20
50	9.8066	9.8853	9.9212	10.0788	10
40° 00'	9.8081	9.8843	9.9238	10.0762	50° 00'
10	9.8096	9.8832	9.9264	10.0736	50
20	9.8111	9.8821	9.9289	10.0711	40
30	9.8125	9.8810	9.9315	10.0685	30
40	9.8140	9.8800	9.9341	10.0659	20
50	9.8155	9.8789	9.9366	10.0634	10
41° 00'	9.8169	9.8778	9.9392	10.0608	49° 00'
10	9.8184	9.8767	9.9417	10.0583	50
20	9.8198	9.8756	9.9443	10.0557	40
30	9.8213	9.8745	9.9468	10.0532	30
40	9.8227	9.8733	9.9494	10.0506	20
50	9.8241	9.8722	9.9519	10.0481	10
42° 00'	9.8255	9.8711	9.9544	10.0456	48° 00'
10	9.8269	9.8699	9.9570	10.0430	50
20	9.8283	9.8688	9.9595	10.0405	40
30	9.8297	9.8676	9.9621	10.0379	30
40	9.8311	9.8665	9.9646	10.0354	20
50	9.8324	9.8653	9.9671	10.0329	10
43° 00'	9.8338	9.8641	9.9697	10.0303	47° 00'
10	9.8351	9.8629	9.9722	10.0278	50
20	9.8365	9.8618	9.9747	10.0253	40
30	9.8378	9.8606	9.9772	10.0228	30
40	9.8391	9.8594	9.9798	10.0202	20
50	9.8405	9.8582	9.9823	10.0177	10
44° 00'	9.8418	9.8569	9.9848	10.0152	46° 00'
10	9.8431	9.8557	9.9874	10.0126	50
20	9.8444	9.8545	9.9899	10.0101	40
30	9.8457	9.8532	9.9924	10.0076	30
40	9.8469	9.8520	9.9949	10.0051	20
50	9.8482	9.8507	9.9975	10.0025	10
45° 00'	9.8495	9.8495	10.0000	10.0000	45° 00'
	L Cos	L Sin	L Cot	L Tan	Angle

* These tables give the logarithms increased by 10. Hence in each case 10 should be subtracted.

Practice Test 2

Part I

Answer 30 questions from this part. Each correct answer will receive 2 credits. No partial credit will be allowed. Write your answers in the spaces provided on the separate answer sheet. Where applicable, answers may be left in terms of π or in radical form.   [60]

1 If $a \circ b$ is defined as $a^2 - 2b$, find the value of $5 \circ 7$.

2 If $\tan A = 1.3400$, find the measure of $\angle A$ to the *nearest degree*.

3 What is the identity element in the system defined by the table below?

★	2	4	6	8
2	4	8	2	6
4	8	6	4	2
6	2	4	6	8
8	6	2	8	4

4 In the accompanying figure, $\overline{DE} \parallel \overline{BC}$, $AD = 10$, $AB = 24$, and $AC = 36$. Find AE.

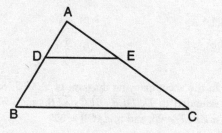

5 Evaluate: $_7C_3$

6 If one of the roots of the equation $x^2 + kx = 6$ is 2, what is the value of k?

7 Solve for the positive value of y: $\dfrac{16}{y} = \dfrac{y}{4}$

8 How many different 4-letter arrangements can be formed from the letters in the word "NINE"?

9 In $\triangle ABC$, $m\angle B > m\angle C$ and $m\angle C > m\angle A$. Which side of $\triangle ABC$ is the longest?

10 In the accompanying diagram of rhombus $ABCD$, diagonal $\overline{AC}$ is drawn. If $m\angle CAB = 35$, find $m\angle ADC$.

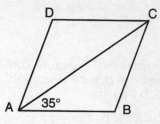

11 What is the slope of the line whose equation is $3x + y = 4$?

12 The graph of the equation $x^2 + y^2 = 9$ represents the locus of points at a given distance, d, from the origin. Find the value of d.

13 Find the area of the parallelogram whose vertices are $(2,1)$, $(7,1)$, $(9,5)$, and $(4,5)$.

14 Express $\dfrac{5x}{6} - \dfrac{x}{3}$ in simplest form.

15 The line that passes through points $(1,3)$ and $(2,y)$ has a slope of 2. What is the value of y?

16 What is the length of a side of a square whose diagonal measures $4\sqrt{2}$?

Directions (17–35): For *each* question chosen, write on the separate answer sheet the *numeral* preceding the word or expression that best completes the statement or answers the question.

17 When factored completely, $x^3 - 9x$ is equivalent to
(1) $x(x - 3)$ (3) $(x + 3)(x - 3)$
(2) $x(x + 3)(x - 3)$ (4) $x(x + 3)$

18 If $(x + 2)^2 + (y - 3)^2 = 25$ is an equation of a circle whose center is $(-2,k)$, then k equals
(1) 1   (3) 3
(2) 2   (4) 4

19 In the accompanying diagram of $\triangle ABC$, side $\overline{BC}$ is extended to D, $m\angle B = 2y$, $m\angle BCA = 6y$, and $m\angle ACD = 3y$.

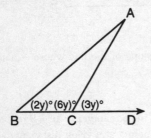

What is $m\angle A$?
(1) 15   (3) 20
(2) 17   (4) 24

20 The coordinates of $\triangle ABC$ are $A(0,0)$, $B(6,0)$, and $C(0,4)$. What are the coordinates of the point at which the median from vertex A intersects side $\overline{BC}$?
(1) $(1,4)$ (3) $(3,0)$
(2) $(2,3)$ (4) $(3,2)$

21 Which statement is the equivalent of $\sim(\sim m \wedge n)$?
(1) $m \wedge n$ (3) $m \vee \sim n$
(2) $m \wedge \sim n$ (4) $\sim m \vee \sim n$

22 The translation $(x,y) \rightarrow (x - 2, y + 3)$ maps the point $(7,2)$ onto the point whose coordinates are
(1) $(9,5)$ (3) $(5,-1)$
(2) $(5,5)$ (4) $(-14,6)$

23 In the accompanying diagram, $\triangle FUN$ is a right triangle, $\overline{UR}$ is the altitude to hypotenuse $\overline{FN}$, $UR = 12$, and the lengths of $\overline{FR}$ and $\overline{RN}$ are in the ratio 1:9.

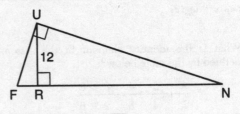

What is the length of $\overline{FR}$?
(1) 1   (3) 36
(2) $1\frac{1}{3}$ (4) 4

24 Lines ℓ and m are perpendicular. The slope of ℓ is $\frac{3}{5}$. What is the slope of m?
(1) $-\frac{3}{5}$ (3) $\frac{3}{5}$
(2) $-\frac{5}{3}$ (4) $\frac{5}{3}$

25 In the accompanying diagram of $\triangle ABC$, $\overline{AC}$ is extended to D, $\overline{DEF}$, $\overline{BEC}$, $\overline{AFB}$, $m\angle B = 50$, $m\angle BEF = 25$, and $m\angle ACB = 65$.

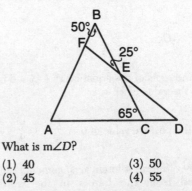

What is $m\angle D$?
(1) 40   (3) 50
(2) 45   (4) 55

120

26 In the accompanying diagram, parallel lines ℓ and m are cut by transversal t.

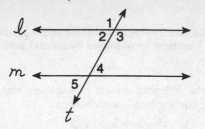

Which statement is true?

(1) m∠1 + m∠2 + m∠5 = 360
(2) m∠1 + m∠2 + m∠3 = 180
(3) m∠1 + m∠2 = m∠2 + m∠3
(4) m∠1 + m∠3 = m∠4 + m∠5

27 Which argument below is *not* valid?

(1) Given: $a \rightarrow b$
  a
  Conclusion: b
(2) Given: $a \vee b$
  $\sim b$
  Conclusion: $\sim a$
(3) Given: $a \rightarrow b$
  $\sim b$
  Conclusion: $\sim a$
(4) Given: $a \rightarrow b$
  $b \rightarrow \sim c$
  Conclusion: $a \rightarrow \sim c$

28 The measure of a base angle of an isosceles triangle is 4 times the measure of the vertex angle. The number of degrees in the vertex angle is

(1) 20   (3) 36
(2) 30   (4) 135

29 What are the coordinates of R', the image of $R(-4,3)$ after a reflection in the line whose equation is $y = x$?

(1) (−4,−3)   (3) (4,3)
(2) (3,−4)   (4) (−3,4)

30 The equation $y = 4$ represents the locus of points that are equidistant from which two points?

(1) (0,0) and (0,8)   (3) (4,0) and (0,4)
(2) (0,3) and (0,1)   (4) (4,4) and (−4,4)

31 In equilateral triangle ABC, $\overline{AD}$ is drawn to $\overline{BC}$ such that $BD < DC$. Which inequality is true?

(1) $DC > AC$ (3) $AD > AB$
(2) $BD > AD$ (4) $AC > AD$

32 Which equation represents the axis of symmetry of the graph of the equation $y = 2x^2 + 7x - 5$?

(1) $x = -\frac{5}{4}$ (3) $x = \frac{7}{4}$

(2) $x = \frac{5}{4}$ (4) $x = -\frac{7}{4}$

33 How many congruent triangles are formed by connecting the midpoints of the three sides of a scalene triangle?

(1) 1   (3) 3
(2) 2   (4) 4

34 What are the roots of the equation $2x^2 - 7x + 4 = 0$?

(1) $\frac{7 \pm \sqrt{17}}{4}$ (3) $4, -\frac{1}{2}$

(2) $\frac{-7 \pm \sqrt{17}}{4}$ (4) $-4, \frac{1}{2}$

35 In the accompanying diagram of quadrilateral $QRST$, $\overline{RS} \cong \overline{ST}$, $\overline{SR} \perp \overline{QR}$, and $\overline{ST} \perp \overline{QT}$.

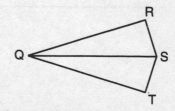

Which method of proof may be used to prove $\triangle QRS \cong \triangle QTS$?

(1) HL   (3) AAS
(2) SAS   (4) ASA

Answers to the following questions are to be written on paper provided by the school.

Part II

Answer three questions from this part. Clearly indicate the necessary steps, including appropriate formula substitutions, diagrams, graphs, charts, etc. Calculations that may be obtained by mental arithmetic or the calculator do not need to be shown. **[30]**

36 Answer *a*, *b*, and *c* for all values of *x* for which these expressions are defined.

  a Find the value of $\dfrac{(x+1)^2}{x^2-1}$ if *x* = 1.02.   **[2]**

  b Find the positive value of *x* to the *nearest thousandth*:

$$\frac{1}{x} = \frac{x+1}{1} \qquad \textbf{[5]}$$

  c Solve for all values of *x* in simplest radical form:

$$\frac{x+2}{4} = \frac{2}{x-2} \qquad \textbf{[3]}$$

37 Triangle *ABC* has coordinates *A*(1,0), *B*(7,4), and *C*(5,7).

  a On graph paper, draw and label $\triangle ABC$.   **[1]**

  b Graph and state the coordinates of $\triangle A'B'C'$, the image of $\triangle ABC$ after a reflection in the origin.   **[3]**

  c Graph and state the coordinates of $\triangle A''B''C''$, the image of $\triangle A'B'C'$ under the translation $(x,y) \rightarrow (x+1, y+5)$.   **[3]**

  d Write an equation of the line containing $\overline{A''B''}$.   **[3]**

38 Solve the following system of equations algebraically or graphically and check:

$$\begin{aligned} y &= x^2 - 6x + 5 \\ y + 7 &= 2x \end{aligned} \qquad \textbf{[8,2]}$$

39 In the accompanying diagram of rhombus *ABCD*, m∠*CAB* = 25 and *AC* = 18.

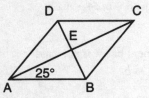

Find, to the *nearest tenth*, the

  a perimeter of *ABCD*   **[6]**

  b length of $\overline{BD}$ **[4]**

40 The vertices of $\triangle NYS$ are *N*(–2,–1), *Y*(0,10), and *S*(10,5). The coordinates of point *T* are (4,2).

  a Prove that $\overline{YT}$ is a median.   **[2]**

  b Prove that $\overline{YT}$ is an altitude.   **[4]**

  c Find the area of $\triangle NYS$.   **[4]**

☞ GO RIGHT ON TO THE NEXT PAGE.

'Answers to the following questions are to be written on paper provided by the school.

Part III

Answer one question from this part. Clearly indicate the necessary steps, including appropriate formula substitutions, diagrams, graphs, charts, etc. Calculations that may be obtained by mental arithmetic or the calculator do not need to be shown.   [10]

41 Given: $\angle 1 \cong \angle 2$ and $\overline{DB} \perp \overline{AC}$.

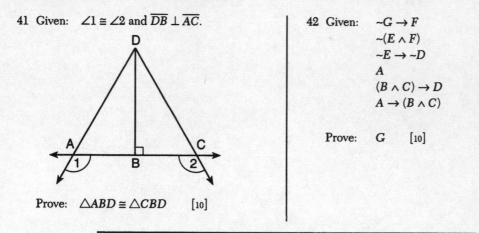

Prove: $\triangle ABD \cong \triangle CBD$ [10]

42 Given: $\sim G \rightarrow F$
$\sim(E \wedge F)$
$\sim E \rightarrow \sim D$
A
$(B \wedge C) \rightarrow D$
$A \rightarrow (B \wedge C)$

Prove: G [10]

Practice Test 2

Answers

1. The correct answer is 11.

   $5 * 7 = (5)^2 - 2(7) = 25 - 14 = 11$

2. The correct answer is 53.

   tan A = 1.3400

   $\tan^{-1}(\tan A) = \tan^{-1}(1.3400) = 53.27$

3. The correct answer is 6 because 6 * any element yields that element.

4. The correct answer is 15.

   Since $\overline{DE}\|\overline{BC}$, $\dfrac{AD}{AB} = \dfrac{AE}{AC}$, so

   $\dfrac{10}{24} = \dfrac{AE}{36}$ Cross multiply.

   $360 = 24AE$ Divide both sides by 24.

   $15 = AE$

5. The correct answer is 35.

   $_7C_3 =$

   $\dfrac{7!}{3!(7-3)!} = \dfrac{7!}{3!4!} = \dfrac{7 \cdot 6 \cdot 5 \cdot 4!}{3 \cdot 2 \cdot 1 \cdot 4!} = 35$

6. The correct answer is 1.

   $(2)^2 + 2k = 6$

   $4 + 2k = 6$ Subtract 4 from both sides.

   $2k = 2$ Divide both sides by 2.

   $k = 1$

7. The correct answer is 8.

   $\dfrac{16}{y} = \dfrac{y}{4}$ Cross multiply.

   $y = \sqrt{64}$ or $y = -\sqrt{64}$

   $y = \pm 8$

   The positive value y of is 8.

8. The correct answer is 12.

   There are 4 ways for first choice, 3 ways for second, etcetera. So $4 \cdot 3 \cdot 2 \cdot 1 = 24$. We must divide by $2! = 2$ since there are two letter N's.

   Thus $\dfrac{24}{2} = 12$.

9. The correct answers is $\overline{AC}$.

   $\angle B$ is the largest angle and the largest side is opposite $\angle B$.

10. The correct answer is 110.

    $AB = BC$ since all sides have the same measure in a rhombus. In isosceles $\triangle ACB$, $m\angle BAC = m\angle ACB = 35$. $m\angle ABC = 180 - (35 + 35) = 110$.

    $\triangle ADC \cong \triangle ABC$, so $m\angle ADC = 110$.

11. The correct answer is -3.

    Solve for y and the coefficient of x is the slope.

    $3x + y = 4$ Subtract $3x$.

    $y = -3x + 4$

12. The correct answer is 3.

    The value of d is $\sqrt{9} = 3$.

13. The correct answer is 20.

    The base is 5 because $7 - 2 = 5$ (or $9 - 4 = 5$)

    The height is 4 because $5 - 1 = 4$.
    The area is $5 \times 4 = 20$

14. The correct answers is $\dfrac{x}{2}$.

    Rewrite with a common denominator of 6.

    $$\frac{5x}{6} - \frac{x}{3} = \frac{5x}{6} - \frac{2x}{6} = \frac{3x}{6} = \frac{x}{2}$$

15. The correct answer is 5.

    Slope is $\dfrac{y - 3}{2 - 1} = y - 3$

    Thus, $y - 3 = 2$ Add 2 to both sides.

    $y = 5$

16. The correct answer is 4.

    Use the Pythagorean Theorem and the fact that the lengths of the sides of a square are equal. Let s be the length of a side.

    $s^2 + s^2 = (4\sqrt{2})^2$

    $2s^2 = 32$ Divide both sides by 2.

    $s^2 = 16$ Take the positive square root of both sides.

    $s = 4$

17. The correct answer is (2).

    $x^3 - 9x = x(x^2 - 9) = x(x + 3)(x - 3)$

18. The correct answer is (3).

    k is the value that makes $y - 3 = 0$, thus $k = 3$.

19. The correct answer is (3).

    Since $\angle BCA$ and $\angle ACD$ form a linear pair,

    $6y + 3y = 180$

    $9y = 180$ Divide both sides by 9.

    $y = 20$

    Then $2y = 40$ and $6y = 120$. The sum of the angles of $\triangle ABC$ is 180. So $40 + 120 + m\angle A = 180$. $160 + m\angle A = 180$, so $m\angle A = 20$.

20. The correct answer is (4).

    It will intersect at the midpoint of (6, 0) and

    (0, 4) which is $\left(\dfrac{6+0}{2}, \dfrac{0+4}{2}\right)$ or (3, 2).

21. The correct answer is (3).

    The negation of ~m is m, and the negation of $p \wedge q$ is ~$p \vee$ ~q. Thus, ~(~$m \wedge n$) is $m \vee$ ~n.

22. The correct answer is (2).

    $(7, 2) \rightarrow (7 - 2, 2 + 3) = (5, 5)$

23. The correct answer is (4).

    ΔFRU is similar to ΔURN, so $\dfrac{FR}{RU} = \dfrac{RU}{RN}$.

    We know the ratio of FR to RN is 1:9 so let $FR = x$ and $RN = 9x$. Thus,

    $\dfrac{x}{12} = \dfrac{12}{9x}$ Cross multiply.

    $9x^2 = 144$

    $x^2 = 16$ Take the positive square
    root of each side.

    $x = 4$

24. The correct answer is (2).

    Perpendicular lines have slopes that are negative reciprocals, the negative reciprocal of $\dfrac{3}{5}$ is $-\dfrac{5}{3}$.

25. The correct answer is (1).

    Since $\angle BEF$ and $\angle CED$ are vertical angles, m$\angle CED = 25°$. $\angle ACB$ and $\angle ECD$ are a linear pair, $65 + m\angle ECD = 180$, thus m$\angle ECD = 115$. The angles of ΔCED add to 180, so $25 + 115 + m\angle D = 180$. $140 + m\angle D = 180$, so m$\angle D = 40$.

26. The correct answer is (3).

    Because both pairs of angles are a linear pair and have the sum of 180.

27. The correct answer is (2).

    Given a or b so not b does not have a valid conclusion of not a.

28. The correct answer is (1).

    There are two equal base angles in an isoscetes triangle, so $4x + 4x + x = 180$; $9x = 180$; $x = 20$.

29. The correct answer is (2).

    Interchange x and y values.

30. The correct answer is (1).

    A line which is equidistant from two points must pass through the midpoint of the two points.

31. The correct answer is (4).

    In ΔADC, m$\angle C = 60$, m$\angle DAC < 60$ since $\angle BAC = 60$. Thus, m$\angle ADC > 60$. Therefore, in ΔADC, $\angle ADC$ is the largest angle and thus, AC is the largest side.

32. The correct answer is (4).

$$y = 2\left(x + \frac{7}{4}\right)^2 - 12\frac{1}{4}$$

The axis of symmetry of the graph with equation $y = ax^2 + bx + c$ is the line with the equation $x = -\frac{b}{2a}$. Here, $a = 2$ and $b = 7$, so the equation of the axis of symmetry is $x = \frac{7}{2(2)}$, or $x = \frac{7}{4}$.

33. The correct answer is (4).

Using the fact that a line segment which connects the midpoints of two sides of a triangle is parallel to the third side and equal in length to half the length of the side it is parallel to, the triangle whose vertices are the midpoints of the sides of the original triangle can be shown to be congruent to each of the other small triangles by SAS.

34. The correct answer is (1).

Use the quadratic formula with $a = 2$, $b = -7$ and $c = 4$.

$$x = \frac{7 \pm \sqrt{49 - 4(2)(4)}}{2(2)}$$

$$x = \frac{7 \pm \sqrt{49 - 32}}{4}$$

$$x = \frac{7 \pm \sqrt{17}}{4}$$

35. The correct answer is (1).

Because $\overline{QS} \cong \overline{QS}$, $\overline{RS} \cong \overline{ST}$ and $\angle R$ and $\angle T$ are right angles.

36. a. The correct answer is 101.

$$\frac{(1.02 + 1)^2}{(1.02)^2 - 1} = \frac{(2.02)^2}{1.0404 - 1} = \frac{4.0804}{.0404} = 101$$

b. The correct answer is 0.618.

$$\frac{1}{x} = \frac{x + 1}{1} \qquad \text{Cross multiply.}$$

$$x(x + 1) = 1$$

$$x^2 + x = 1$$

$$x^2 + x - 1 = 0 \qquad \text{Use quadratic formula for } a = 1, b = 1, c = -1$$

$$x = \frac{-1 \pm \sqrt{1 - 4(1)(-1)}}{2(1)} = \frac{-1 \pm \sqrt{1 + 4}}{2} = \frac{-1 \pm \sqrt{5}}{2}$$

$$\frac{-1 + \sqrt{5}}{2} = .618 \qquad \frac{-1 - \sqrt{5}}{2} = -1.618$$

c. The correct answer is $\pm 2\sqrt{3}$.

$$\frac{x + 2}{4} = \frac{2}{x - 2} \qquad \text{Cross multiply.}$$

$$(x + 2)(x - 2) = 8$$

$$x^2 - 4 = 8 \qquad \text{Add 4 to both sides.}$$

$$x^2 = 12$$

$$x = \pm\sqrt{12} = \pm\sqrt{4}\sqrt{3} = \pm 2\sqrt{3}$$

37. a.

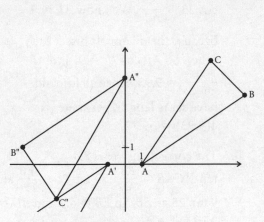

b. $A'(-1, 0)$, $B'(-7, -4)$, $C'(-5, -7)$

Change the signs of the coordinates.

c. $A''(0, 5)$ $B''(-6, 1)$ $C''(-4, -2)$

$(-1, 0) \rightarrow (-1 + 1, 0 + 5) \rightarrow (0, 5)$ A''.

$(-7, -4) \rightarrow (-7 + 1, -4 + 5) \rightarrow (-6, 1)$ B''.

$(-5, -7) \rightarrow (-5 + 1, -7 + 5) \rightarrow (-4, -2)$ C''.

d. $y = \dfrac{2}{3} x + 5$

Slope $= \dfrac{1 - 5}{-6 - 0} = \dfrac{-4}{-6} = \dfrac{4}{6} = \dfrac{2}{3}$

Using the point slope formula with $(0, 5)$

$y - 5 = \dfrac{2}{3} (x - 0)$

$y - 5 = \dfrac{2}{3} x$ Add 5 to both sides.

$y = \dfrac{2}{3} x + 5$

38. $(6, 5)$ and $(2, -3)$

Solve $y + 7 = 2x$ for y

$y = 2x - 7$

Substitute into $y = x^2 - 6x + 5$

$2x - 7 = x^2 - 6x + 5$

$0 = x^2 - 8x + 12$ Factor

$0 = (x - 6)(x - 2)$ Set each factor
                                      equal to 0

$x - 6 = 0$ $x - 2 = 0$

$x = 6$ $x = 2$

Substitute into $y = 2x - 7$

$y = 2(6) - 7$ $y = 2(2) - 7$

$y = 12 - 7$ $y = 4 - 7$

$y = 5$ $y = -3$

$(6, 5)$ $(2, -3)$

Check:

First check $(6, 5)$.

$5 = 6^2 - 6(6) + 5$

$5 = 36 - 36 + 5$

$5 = 5 \checkmark$

$5 + 7 = 2(6)$

$5 + 7 = 12$

$12 = 12 \checkmark$

Now check $(2, -3)$

$-3 = 2^2 - 6(2) + 5$

$-3 = 4 - 12 + 5$

$-3 = -3 \checkmark$

$-3 + 7 = 2(2)$

$4 = 4 \checkmark$

Graphically the solution is this:

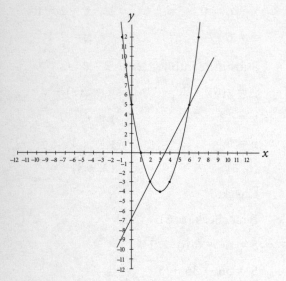

It is seen that the solutions are $(6, 5)$ and $(2, -3)$.

Checking these solutions is the same as with the algebraic solution.

39. a. The correct answer is 39.7

$\triangle AEB$ is a triangle, and using the fact that the $\cos \angle CAB = \dfrac{AE}{AB}$, we have $\cos 25 = \dfrac{9}{AB}$. We know $AE = 9$ because the diagonals bisect each other. So $AB \cos 25 = 9$, and $AB = \dfrac{9}{\cos 25} = 9.93$. Since all four sides have same length, perimeter is $4(9.93) = 39.72$.

b. The correct answer is 8.4

$\tan \angle CAB = \dfrac{EB}{AE}$. So $\tan 25 = \dfrac{EB}{9}$ and $9 \tan 25 = EB$. So $EB = 4.2$ and $BD = 2EB = 8.4$

40. a. The median should go to the midpoint of NS.

The midpoint is

$\left(\dfrac{-2 + 10}{2}, \dfrac{-1 + 5}{2} \right) = \left(\dfrac{8}{2}, \dfrac{4}{2} \right) = (4, 2)$.

These are the coordinates of T.

b. $\overline{YT}$ intersects $\overline{NS}$. Need to show that $\overline{YT}$ is perpendicular to $\overline{NS}$.

Slope of $\overline{NS} = \dfrac{5 - (-1)}{10 - (-2)} = \dfrac{6}{12} = \dfrac{1}{2}$

Slope of $YT = \dfrac{2 - 10}{4 - 0} = \dfrac{-8}{4} = -2$

These are negative reciprocals so the lines are perpendicular.

c. $YT =$

$\sqrt{(4-0)^2 + (2-10)^2} = \sqrt{4^2 + (-8)^2} =$

$\sqrt{16 + 64} = \sqrt{80} = \sqrt{16} \cdot \sqrt{5} = 4\sqrt{5}$

$NS =$

$\sqrt{[10 - (-2)]^2 + [5 - (-1)]^2} =$
$\sqrt{12^2 + 6^2} =$

$\sqrt{144 + 36} = \sqrt{180} = \sqrt{36} \cdot \sqrt{5} = 6\sqrt{5}$

$\begin{aligned} \text{Area} \quad &= \frac{1}{2}(4\sqrt{5})(6\sqrt{5}) \\ &= \frac{1}{2}(24)(\sqrt{5} \cdot \sqrt{5}) \\ &= 12 \cdot 5 \\ &= 60 \end{aligned}$

41. $\angle DAB$ and $\angle 1$ are a linear pair of angles, so $m\angle DAB + m\angle 1 = 180$ and $m\angle DAB = 180 - m\angle 1$. Similarly $\angle DCB$ and $\angle 2$ are a linear pair and $m\angle DCB + m\angle 2 = 180$, so $m\angle DCB = 180 - m\angle 2$. Since $\angle 1 \cong \angle 2$, $m\angle 1 = m\angle 2$ and thus $m\angle DAB = m\angle DCB$ and $\angle DAB \cong \angle DCB$. Since base angles are congruent, ΔDAC is isosceles with $\overline{AD} \cong \overline{DC}$. Since $\overline{DB} \perp \overline{AC}$, $\angle DBA$ and $\angle DBC$ are right angles and thus congruent. By AAS (or HA) $\Delta ABD \cong \Delta CBD$.

42.

Statements of direct proof	Reasons
1. A	Given
2. $A \rightarrow (B \wedge C)$	Given
3. $B \wedge C$	Law of detachment applied to steps 1 and 2
4. $(B \wedge C) \rightarrow D$	Given
5. D	Law of detachment applied to steps 3 and 4
6. $\sim E \rightarrow \sim D$	Given
7. $D \rightarrow E$	Law of contrapostive applied to step 6
8. E	Law of detachment applied to steps 5 and 7
9. $\sim(E \wedge F)$	Given
10. $\sim E \vee \sim F$	De Morgan's law applied to step 9
11. $\sim F$	Law of disjunctive inference applied to steps 8 and 10
12. $\sim G \rightarrow F$	Given
13. $\sim F \rightarrow G$	Law of contrapositive applied to step 12
14. G	Law of detachment applied to steps 11 and 13

Practice Test 3

Part I

Answer 30 questions from this part. Each correct answer will receive 2 credits. No partial credit will be allowed. Write your answers in the spaces provided on the separate answer sheet. Where applicable, answers may be left in terms of π or in radical form.   [60]

1 Using the accompanying table, solve for x if $x \cdot b = a$.

$\cdot$	a	b	c
a	a	b	c
b	b	a	c
c	c	c	b

2 In the accompanying diagram, $\triangle ABC$ is similar to $\triangle A'B'C'$, $AB = 14.4$, $BC = 8$, $CA = 12$, $A'B' = x$, and $B'C' = 4$. Find the value of x.

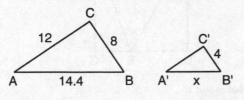

3 In the accompanying diagram, parallel lines $\overleftrightarrow{AB}$ and $\overleftrightarrow{CD}$ are intersected by $\overleftrightarrow{GH}$ at E and F, respectively. If $m\angle BEF = 5x - 10$ and $m\angle CFE = 4x + 20$, find x.

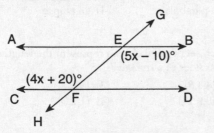

4 If $\tan A = 0.5400$, find the measure of $\angle A$ to the *nearest degree*.

5 Find the length of a side of a square if two consecutive vertices have coordinates $(-2,6)$ and $(6,6)$.

6 In the accompanying diagram of isosceles triangle ABC, $CA = CB$ and $\angle CBD$ is an exterior angle formed by extending $\overline{AB}$ to point D. If $m\angle CBD = 130$, find $m\angle C$.

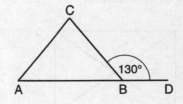

7 If $\overleftrightarrow{AB}$ intersects $\overleftrightarrow{CD}$ at E, $m\angle AEC = 3x$, and $m\angle AED = 5x - 60$, find the value of x.

8 Point (x,y) is the image of $(2,4)$ after a reflection in point $(5,6)$. In which quadrant does (x,y) lie?

9 In the accompanying diagram, $ABCD$ is a parallelogram, $\overline{EC} \perp \overline{DC}$, $\angle B \cong E$, and $m\angle A = 100$. Find $m\angle CDE$.

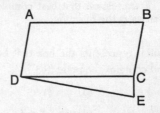

10 The lengths of the sides of $\triangle DEF$ are 6, 8, and 10. Find the perimeter of the triangle formed by connecting the midpoints of the sides of $\triangle DEF$.

11 The coordinates of the midpoint of line segment $\overline{AB}$ are $(1,2)$. If the coordinates of point A are $(1,0)$, find the coordinates of point B.

12 In $\triangle PQR$, $\angle Q \cong \angle R$. If $PQ = 10x - 14$, $PR = 2x + 50$, and $RQ = 4x - 30$, find the value of x.

13 What is the image of $(-2,4)$ after a reflection in the x-axis?

14 In rectangle $ABCD$, $\overline{AC}$ and $\overline{BD}$ are diagonals. If $m\angle 1 = 55$, find $m\angle ABD$.

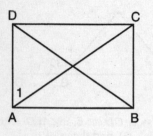

15 What is the slope of the line that passes through points $(-1,5)$ and $(2,3)$?

16 The coordinates of the turning point of the graph of the equation $y = x^2 - 2x - 8$ are $(1,k)$. What is the value of k?

Directions (17–35): For *each* question chosen, write on the separate answer sheet the *numeral* preceding the word or expression that best completes the statement or answers the question.

17 Which equation represents the line that has a slope of $\frac{1}{2}$ and contains the point $(0,3)$?

(1) $y = \frac{1}{3}x + \frac{1}{2}$ (3) $y = \frac{3}{2}x$

(2) $y = 3x + \frac{1}{2}$ (4) $y = \frac{1}{2}x + 3$

18 If the measures of the angles in a triangle are in the ratio 3:4:5, the measure of an exterior angle of the triangle can *not* be

(1) 165° (3) 120°
(2) 135° (4) 105°

19 According to De Morgan's laws, which statement is logically equivalent to $\sim(p \wedge q)$?

(1) $\sim p \vee \sim q$ (3) $\sim p \wedge q$
(2) $\sim p \vee q$ (4) $\sim p \wedge \sim q$

20 One angle of a triangle measures 30°. If the measures of the other two angles are in the ratio 3:7, the measure of the largest angle of the triangle is

(1) 15° (3) 126°
(2) 105° (4) 147°

21 In the accompanying diagram, $ABCD$ is a rectangle, E is a point on $\overline{CD}$, $m\angle DAE = 30$, and $m\angle CBE = 20$.

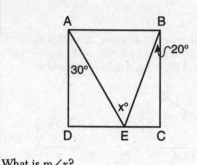

What is $m\angle x$?

(1) 25 (3) 60
(2) 50 (4) 70

22 The graph of the equation $y = ax^2 + bx + c$, $a \neq 0$, forms

(1) a circle (3) a straight line
(2) a parabola (4) an ellipse

23 Which set of numbers can represent the lengths of the sides of a triangle?

(1) {4,4,8} (3) {3,5,7}
(2) {3,9,14} (4) {1,2,3}

24 Which is an equation of the line that passes through point $(3,5)$ and is parallel to the x-axis?

(1) $x = 3$ (3) $y = 5$
(2) $x = 5$ (4) $y = 3$

25 What are the factors of $y^3 - 4y$?

(1) $y(y - 2)(y - 2)$ (3) $(y^2 + 1)(y - 4)$
(2) $y(y + 4)(y - 4)$ (4) $y(y + 2)(y - 2)$

26 In the accompanying diagram of right triangle ABC, $AB = 4$ and $BC = 7$.

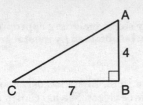

What is the length of $\overline{AC}$ to the *nearest hundredth*?

(1) 5.74   (3) 8.06
(2) 5.75   (4) 8.08

27 Which is the converse of the statement "If today is Presidents' Day, then there is no school"?

(1) If there is school, then today is not Presidents' Day.
(2) If there is no school, then today is Presidents' Day.
(3) If today is Presidents' Day, then there is school.
(4) If today is not Presidents' Day, then there is school.

28 How many different eight-letter permutations can be formed from the letters in the word "PARALLEL"?

(1) $\frac{8!}{3!2!}$ (3) 360

(2) $8!$ (4) $\frac{8!}{3!}$

29 Which equation describes the locus of points equidistant from $A(-3,2)$ and $B(-3,8)$?

(1) $x = -3$ (3) $x = 5$
(2) $y = -3$ (4) $y = 5$

30 A translation maps $A(1,2)$ onto $A'(-1,3)$. What are the coordinates of the image of the origin under the same translation?

(1) $(0,0)$ (3) $(-2,1)$
(2) $(2,-1)$ (4) $(-1,2)$

31 The solution set of the equation $x^2 + 5x = 0$ is

(1) $\{0\}$ (3) $\{-5\}$
(2) $\{5\}$ (4) $\{0,-5\}$

32 In the accompanying diagram of parallelogram $MATH$, $m\angle T = 100$ and $\overline{SH}$ bisects $\angle MHT$.

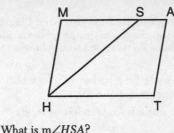

What is $m\angle HSA$?

(1) 80   (3) 120
(2) 100   (4) 140

33 What are the roots of the equation $x^2 + 9x + 12 = 0$?

(1) $\frac{-9 \pm \sqrt{33}}{2}$ (3) $\frac{-9 \pm \sqrt{129}}{2}$

(2) $\frac{9 \pm \sqrt{33}}{2}$ (4) $\frac{9 \pm \sqrt{129}}{2}$

34 The vertices of trapezoid $ABCD$ are $A(-3,0)$, $B(-3,4)$, $C(2,4)$, and $D(4,0)$. What is the area of trapezoid $ABCD$?

(1) 6   (3) 28
(2) 24   (4) 48

35 The accompanying diagram shows how $\triangle A'B'C'$ is constructed similar to $\triangle ABC$.

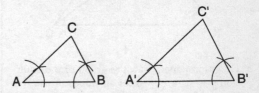

Which statement proves the construction?

(1) If two triangles are congruent, they are similar.
(2) If two triangles are similar, the angles of one triangle are congruent to the corresponding angles of the other triangle.
(3) Two triangles are similar if two angles of one triangle are congruent to two angles of the other triangle.
(4) The corresponding sides of two similar triangles are proportional.

Answers to the following questions are to be written on paper provided by the school.

Part II

Answer three questions from this part. Clearly indicate the necessary steps, including appropriate formula substitutions, diagrams, graphs, charts, etc. Calculations that may be obtained by mental arithmetic or the calculator do not need to be shown. [30]

36 Answer both *a* and *b* for all values of *y* for which these expressions are defined.

a Express as a single fraction in lowest terms:

$$\frac{y-4}{2y} + \frac{3y-5}{5y} \quad [4]$$

b Simplify:

$$\frac{y^2 - 7y + 10}{5y - y^2} \div \frac{y^2 - 4}{25y^3} \quad [6]$$

37 In the accompanying diagram of isosceles triangle *KLC*, $\overline{LK} \cong \overline{LC}$, m∠*K* = 53, altitude $\overline{CA}$ is drawn to leg $\overline{LK}$, and *LA* = 3. Find the perimeter of △ *KLC* to the *nearest integer*. [10]

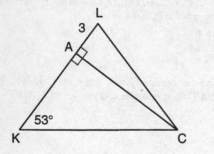

38 *a* On graph paper, draw the graph of the equation $y = -x^2 + 6x - 8$ for all values of *x* in the interval $0 \le x \le 6$. [6]

b What is the maximum value of *y* in the equation $y = -x^2 + 6x - 8$? [2]

c Write an equation of the line that passes through the turning point and is parallel to the *x*-axis. [2]

39 At a video rental store, Elyssa has only enough money to rent three videos. She has chosen four comedies, six dramas, and one mystery movie to consider.

a How many different selections of three videos may she rent from the movies she has chosen? [2]

b How many selections of three videos will consist of one comedy and two dramas? [3]

c What is the probability that a selection of three videos will consist of one of each type of video? [3]

d Elyssa decides to rent one comedy, one drama, and one mystery movie. In how many different orders may she view these videos? [2]

40 In the accompanying diagram of right triangle *ABC*, altitude $\overline{BD}$ is drawn to hypotenuse $\overline{AC}$, *AC* = 20, *AD* < *DC*, and *BD* = 6.

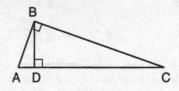

a If *AD* = *x*, express *DC* in terms of *x*. [1]

b Solve for *x*. [6]

c Find *AB* in simplest radical form. [3]

☞ GO RIGHT ON TO THE NEXT PAGE.

Answers to the following questions are to be written on paper provided by the school.

Part III

Answer one question from this part. Clearly indicate the necessary steps, including appropriate formula substitutions, diagrams, graphs, charts, etc. Calculations that may be obtained by mental arithmetic or the calculator do not need to be shown.　[10]

41 Given: $\triangle ABC$; $\overline{BD}$ is both the median and the altitude to $\overline{AC}$.

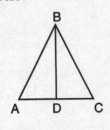

Prove: $\overline{BA} \cong \overline{BC}$　[10]

42 Quadrilateral $ABCD$ has vertices $A(-6,3)$, $B(-3,6)$, $C(9,6)$, and $D(-5,-8)$. Prove that quadrilateral $ABCD$ is

a a trapezoid　[6]

b *not* an isosceles trapezoid　[4]

Practice Test 3

Answers

1. The correct answer is b.

   Look in either the row or column of b to find the answer. Look then to the column or row to find x.

2. The correct answer is 7.2.

   $$\frac{4}{8} = \frac{x}{14.4} \qquad \text{Cross multiply.}$$

   $8x = 57.6$

   $x = 7.2$

3. The correct answer is $x = 30$.

   Since these are alternate interior angles and the lines are parallel,

   $4x + 20 = 5x - 10$

   $30 = x$

4. The correct answer is 28.

   $\tan A = 0.5400$

   $\tan^{-1}(\tan A) = \tan^{-1}(.5400)$

   $A = 28.369$

5. Since the y-coordinates are the same, the length is found by finding the positive difference of the x-coordinates. So the length is $6 - (-2) = 6 + 2 = 8$.

6. The correct answer is 80°.

   $m\angle CBA = 50$ since $m\angle CBA + m\angle CBD = 180$. Since $CA = CB$, then $m\angle A = m\angle CBA = 50$. $m\angle A + m\angle C\, m\angle CBA = 180$. So $50 + m\angle C + 50 = 180$ and $m\angle C = 80$.

7. The correct answer is 30.

   $\angle AED$ and $\angle AEC$ are a linear pair of angles, so

   $3x + 5x - 60 = 180$

   $8x - 60 = 180 \qquad \text{Add 60 to both sides.}$

   $8x = 240 \qquad \text{Divide both sides by 8.}$

   $x = 30$

8. The correct answer is I.

   Reflecting $(2, 4)$ about $(5, 6)$ will not change the quadrant and $(2, 4)$ is in quadrant I.

9. The correct answer is 10.

   Consecutive angles in a parallelogram are supplementary. Since $m\angle A = 100$, $m\angle B = 80$ and thus $m\angle E = 80$. In $\triangle CDE$ the sum of the angles is 180°, so $90 + 80 + m\angle CDE = 180$ and $m\angle CDE = 10$.

10. The correct answer is 12.

    If a line segment connects the midpoints of two sides of a triangle, it is parallel to the third side and has a length half of the length of the third side. So the perimeter of the triangle formed is $\frac{1}{2}(6) + \frac{1}{2}(8) + \frac{1}{2}(10)$

    $= 3 + 4 + 5 = 12$

11. The correct answer is $(1, 4)$

    The midpoint of $A(1, 0)$ and $B(x, y)$ would be $\left(\frac{1 + x}{2}, \frac{0 + y}{2}\right)$. Thus,

    $\frac{1 + x}{2} = 1$ and $\frac{0 + y}{2} = 2$ Cross multiply.

    $1 + x = 2$ $0 + y = 4$

    $x = 1$ $y = 4$

12. The correct answer is 8.

    Since $\angle Q \cong \angle R$, then $\overline{PR} \cong \overline{PQ}$ and $PR = PQ$ so

    $2x + 50 = 10x - 14$

    $64 = 8x$ Divide both sides by 8.

    $8 = x$

13. $(-2, -4)$

    Change the sign of the y-value.

14. The correct answer is 35.

    The $m\angle DAB = 90$, so $m\angle CAB = 35$. If we label the intersection of the diagonals E, then $AE = EB$, since the diagonals are congruent and bisect each other. Thus, $m\angle CAB = m\angle ABD$.

15. The correct answer is $\frac{-2}{3}$.

    $\text{slope} = \frac{3 - 5}{2 - (-1)} = \frac{-2}{3}$

16. The correct answer is -9.

    Substitute in 1 for x and solve for y.

    $y = (1)^2 - 2(1) - 8 = 1 - 2 - 8 = -9$

17. The correct answer is (4).

    When equation is in the form $y = mx + b$, m is the slope and b is the value when $x = 0$.

18. The correct answer is (1).

    If the ratio is 3:4:5 then there are 12 equal parts. The angle total of 180° divided by 12 equals 15. So the angles are $3(15) = 45°$, $4(15) = 60°$ and $5(15) = 75°$. Thus the exterior angles are 135°, 120°, and 105°.

19. The correct answer is (1).

    Negate both statements and change $\wedge$ to $\vee$.

20. The correct answer is (2).

    If one angle measures 30°, the other 2 have a sum of 150°. The ratio of 3:7 says there are 10 equal parts, so each parts is $\frac{150}{10} = 15$.

    The largest angle is 7 parts, $7(15) = 105$.

21. The correct answer is (2).

    Since $ABCD$ is a rectangle, m$\angle DAB = 90$ and m$\angle ABC = 90$. Thus, m$\angle DAE +$ m$\angle EAB = 90$, $30 + $ m$\angle EAB = 90$, m$\angle EAB = 60$. Similarly, m$\angle ABE = 70$. In $\triangle AEB$ the sum of the angles is 180, so $70° + 60° + x°$ $= 180°$ and $x = 50$.

22. The correct answer is (2).

    Since only one variable is squared.

23. The correct answer is (3).

    Since the sum of the smallest two sides is greater than the largest side.

24. The correct answer is (3).

    All lines parallel to the x-axis are $y =$ number. The y-value is 5.

25. The correct answer is (4).

    $y^3 - 4y = y(y^2 - 4) = y(y + 2)(y - 2)$.

26. The correct answer is (3).

    $(AC)^2 = 4^2 + 7^2$

    $(AC)^2 = 16 + 49$

    $(AC)^2 = 65$

    $AC = \sqrt{65} \approx 8.06$

27. The correct answer is (2).

    Interchange the if-then parts.

28. The correct answer is (1).

    $\frac{8!}{3!2!}$ The 8! because there are 8 letters,

    the 3! because there are 3 L's, 2! because there are 2 A's.

29. The correct answer is (4).

    Because $\frac{8 + 2}{2} = \frac{10}{2} = 5$ and the x-values are the same.

30. The correct answer is (3).

    1 to -1 is $-1 - 1 = -2$; 2 to 3 is $3 - 2 = 1$

    The translation maps (x, y) to $(x - 2, y + 1)$.

    $(0, 0) \rightarrow (0 - 2, 0 + 1) = (-2, 1)$

31. The correct answer is (4).

    $x^2 + 5x = 0$ Factor the left side.

    $x(x + 5) = 0$ Set each factor equal
    to zero.

    $x = 0$ $x + 5 = 0$

                       $x = -5$

32. The correct answer is (4).

    $m\angle T + m\angle MHT = 180$, so
    $m\angle MHT = 80$. Thus, $m\angle MHS = 40$.
    $m\angle M = m\angle T = 100$.
    Thus, $m\angle MHS + m\angle M + m\angle MSH = 180$
    and $40 + 100 + m\angle MSH = 180$
    and $m\angle MSH = 40$.

    $m\angle MSH + m\angle HSA = 180$, so
    $40 + m\angle HSA = 180$ and $m\angle HSA = 140$.

33. The correct answer is (1).

    $$\frac{-9 \pm \sqrt{9^2 - 4(1)(12)}}{2(1)} = \frac{-9 \pm \sqrt{81 - 48}}{2} =$$

    $$\frac{-9 \pm \sqrt{33}}{2}$$

34. The correct answer is (2).

    The height AB is the distance from $(-3,0)$
    to $(-3,4)$, which is $4 - 0 = 4$.

    The two bases have length,

    $AD = 4 - (-3) = 4 + 3 = 7$

    $BC = 2 - (-3) = 2 + 3 = 5$

    Area $= \frac{1}{2}(4)(5 + 7) = 2(12) = 24$

35. The correct answer is (3).

    Because 2 pairs of congruent angles have
    been constructed.

36. a. $\dfrac{11y - 30}{10y}$

    Rewrite with common denominator of $10y$

    $$\frac{5(y - 4)}{10y} + \frac{2(3y - 5)}{10y} = \frac{5y - 20}{10y} + \frac{6y - 10}{10y}$$

    $$= \frac{11y - 30}{10y}$$

    b. $\dfrac{-25y^2}{y+2}$

    Factor, invert second fraction and cancel
    common factors

    $$\frac{(y-5)(y-2)}{y(5-y)} \cdot \frac{25y^2 y}{(y-2)(y+2)}$$
    $$-1$$

                   Note: $5 - y = -1(y - 5)$

    $$= \frac{25y^2}{-(y+2)} = \frac{-25y^2}{y+2}$$

37. The correct answer is 35.

    $m\angle K + m\angle L + m\angle LCK = 180$ and
    $m\angle K = m\angle LCK = 53$.

    So $53 + m\angle L + 53 = 180$,
    $m\angle L + 106 = 180$, $m\angle L = 74$

    In $\triangle LAC$, $\cos 74° = \dfrac{\text{adj}}{\text{hyp}} = \dfrac{LA}{LC} = \dfrac{3}{LC}$.

    $\cos 74° = \dfrac{3}{LC}$; $LC \cos 74° = 3$;

    $LC = \dfrac{3}{\cos 74°} = 10.88$.

    Since $LC = LK = 10.88$ and $LA = 3$, then
    $AK = 7.88$.

    In $\triangle AKC$, $\cos 53° = \dfrac{\text{adj}}{\text{hyp}} = \dfrac{AK}{KC} = \dfrac{7.88}{KC}$.

    $\cos 53° = \dfrac{7.88}{KC}$; $KC \cos 53° = 7.88$;

    $KC = \dfrac{7.88}{\cos 53°} = 13.09$.

    Perimeter $= 10.88 + 10.88 + 13.09 = 34.85$.

38. a.

x	y
0	$-(0)^2 + 6(0) - 8 = -8$
1	$-(1)^2 + 6(1) - 8 = -1 + 6 - 8 = -3$
2	$-(2)^2 + 6(2) - 8 = -4 + 12 - 8 = 0$
3	$-(3)^2 + 6(3) - 8 = -9 + 18 - 8 = 1$
4	$-(4)^2 + 6(4) - 8 = -16 + 24 - 8 = 0$
5	$-(5)^2 + 6(5) - 8 = -25 + 30 - 8 = -3$
6	$-(6)^2 + 6(6) - 8 = -36 + 36 - 8 = -8$

    b. 1 is the highest y value.

    c. $y = 1$

    The turning point is (3, 1) so the equation is $y = 1$ since all lines parallel to the x-axis have the equation $y = $ number.

    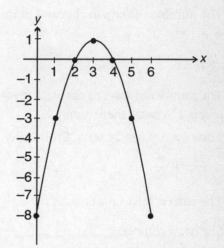

39. a. The correct answer is 165.

    There 11 movies so $_{11}C_3 =$

    $\dfrac{11!}{3!8!} = \dfrac{11 \cdot 10 \cdot 9 \cdot 8!}{3 \cdot 2 \cdot 1 \cdot 8!} = \dfrac{990}{6} = 165$

    b. The correct answer is 60.

    To choose 1 comedy is $_4C_1 =$

    $\dfrac{4!}{3!1!} = \dfrac{4 \cdot 3!}{1 \cdot 3!} = 4$

    To choose 2 dramas is $_6C_2 =$

    $\dfrac{6!}{4!2!} = \dfrac{6 \cdot 5 \cdot 4!}{2 \cdot 1 \cdot 4!} = 15$

    Multiply together $4 \cdot 15 = 60$

c. The correct answer is $\frac{8}{55}$.

The number of ways to choose 1 comedy is $_4C_1 =$

$\frac{4!}{3!1!} = \frac{4 \cdot 3!}{1 \cdot 3!} = 4$

The number of ways to choose 1 drama is $_6C_1 =$

$\frac{6!}{5!1!} = 6$

The number of ways to choose 1 mystery is 1 because there is only 1.

Thus $4 \times 6 \times 1 = 24$ ways. Probability is $\frac{24}{165} = \frac{8}{55}$.

d. The correct answer is 6.

She has 3 choices,

    first movie 3 choices

    second movie 2 choices

    last movie 1 choice.

Thus, $3 \times 2 \times 1 = 6$ ways.

40. a. The correct answer is $20 - x$.

$AC = 20$ and $AC = AD + DC$ so

$20 = x + DC$ and $DC = 20 - x$.

b. The correct answer is 2.

$\triangle ADB$ is similar to $\triangle BDC$ because

$\angle A \cong \angle DBC$ and $\angle ABD \cong \angle C$

Thus, $\frac{AD}{BD} = \frac{BD}{CD}$ $\frac{x}{6} = \frac{6}{20 - x}$

                               Cross multiply.

$x(20 - x) = 36$

$20x - x^2 = 36$

$0 = x^2 - 20x + 36$ Factor the right side.

$0 = (x - 18)(x - 2)$ Set each factor equal to zero.

$x - 18 = 0$ $x - 2 = 0$

$x = 18$ $x = 2$

Since $AD < DC$, $x = 2$

c. The correct answer is $2\sqrt{10}$.

Using $\triangle ABD$

$(AB)^2 = 2^2 + 6^2$

$(AB)^2 = 4 + 36$

$(AB)^2 = 40$

$AB = \sqrt{40} = \sqrt{4} \cdot \sqrt{10} = 2\sqrt{10}$

41. Since $\overline{BD}$ is a median, $\overline{AD} \cong \overline{DC}$. Since $\overline{BD}$ is an altitude, $\overline{BD} \perp \overline{AC}$ and $\angle BDA$ and $\angle BDC$ are right angles. Thus, $\angle BDA \cong \angle BDC$.

Also $\overline{BD} \cong \overline{BD}$. By SAS, $\triangle ABD \cong \triangle CBD$ and $\overline{BA}$ and $\overline{BC}$ are corresponding parts. Thus $\overline{BA} \cong \overline{BC}$.

42. a.

Slope of $AB = \dfrac{6-3}{-3-(-6)} = \dfrac{3}{3} = 1$

Slope of $CD = \dfrac{-8-6}{-5-9} = \dfrac{-14}{-14} = 1$

Slope of $AD = \dfrac{-8-3}{-5-(-6)} = \dfrac{-11}{1} = -11$

Slope of $BC = \dfrac{6-6}{9-(-3)} = \dfrac{0}{12} = 0$

Thus $\overline{AB}$ is parallel to $\overline{CD}$ because they have the same slope, while $\overline{AD}$ is not parallel to $\overline{BC}$ because they have different slopes. So $ABCD$ is a trapezoid.

b. $AD =$

$\sqrt{[-5-(-6)]^2 + (-8-3)^2}$

$= \sqrt{1^2 + (-11)^2}$

$= \sqrt{1+121} = \sqrt{122}$

$BC = 9 - (-3) = 9 + 3 = 12$

Since $AD \neq BC$, $ABCD$ is not an isosceles trapezoid.

Practice Test 4

Answer 30 questions from this part. Each correct answer will receive 2 credits. No partial credit will be allowed. Write your answers in the spaces provided on the separate answer sheet. Where applicable, answers may be left in terms of π or in radical form.   [60]

1 Using the table below, compute $(1 \star 5) \star (2 \star 7)$.

★	1	2	5	7
1	2	7	1	5
2	7	5	2	1
5	1	2	5	7
7	5	1	7	2

2 In the accompanying diagram, line ℓ is parallel to line k, line $m \perp$ line k, and $m\angle x = m\angle y$. Find $m\angle x$.

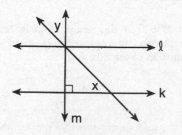

3 If ♥ is a binary operation defined as $a \heartsuit b = \sqrt{a^2 + b^2}$, find the value of $12 \heartsuit 5$.

4 In the accompanying diagram of similar triangles ABE and ACD, $\overline{ABC}$, $\overline{AED}$, $AB = 6$, $BC = 3$, and $ED = 4$. Find the length of $\overline{AE}$.

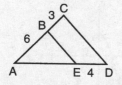

5 How many different 5-letter arrangements can be formed from the letters in the word "DANNY"?

6 Evaluate: $\dfrac{9!}{3!5!}$

7 In the accompanying diagram of $\triangle ABC$, $\overline{AB}$ is extended to E and D, exterior angle CBD measures 130°, and $m\angle C = 75$. Find $m\angle CAE$.

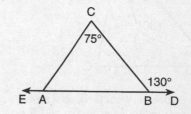

8 In right triangle ABC, $\angle C$ is a right angle and $m\angle B = 60$. What is the ratio of $m\angle A$ to $m\angle B$?

9 In $\triangle ABC$, $m\angle A = 3x + 40$, $m\angle B = 8x + 35$, and $m\angle C = 10x$. Which is the longest side of the triangle?

10 A bookshelf contains seven math textbooks and three science textbooks. If two textbooks are drawn at random without replacement, what is the probability both books are science textbooks?

11 Express the product in lowest terms:

$$\frac{x^2 - x - 6}{3x - 9} \cdot \frac{2}{x + 2}$$

12 In rhombus $ABCD$, the measure of $\angle A$ is 30° more than twice the measure of $\angle B$. Find $m\angle B$.

13 The endpoints of the diameter of a circle are $(-6,2)$ and $(10,-2)$. What are the coordinates of the center of the circle?

14 Find the area of a triangle whose vertices are $(1,2)$, $(8,2)$, and $(1,6)$.

15 Find the distance between points $(-1,-1)$ and $(2,-5)$.

16 In the accompanying diagram, the bisectors of ∠A and ∠B in acute triangle ABC meet at D, and m∠ADB = 130. Find m∠C.

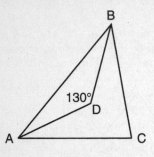

17 Point P is on line m. What is the total number of points 3 centimeters from line m and 5 centimeters from point P?

18 The diagonals of a rhombus are 8 and 10. Find the measure of a side of the rhombus to the *nearest tenth*.

Directions (19–34): For *each* question chosen, write on the separate answer sheet the *numeral* preceding the word or expression that best completes the statement or answers the question.

19 In isosceles triangle ABC, $\overline{AB} \cong \overline{BC}$, point D lies on $\overline{AC}$, and $\overline{BD}$ is drawn. Which inequality is true?
(1) m∠A > m∠ADB
(2) m∠C > m∠CDB
(3) BD > AB
(4) AB > BD

20 If the statements m, m → p, and r → ~p are true, which statement must also be true?
(1) ~r
(2) ~p
(3) r ∧ ~p
(4) ~p ∨ ~m

21 If a point in Quadrant IV is reflected in the y-axis, its image will lie in Quadrant
(1) I
(2) II
(3) III
(4) IV

22 In right triangle ABC, m∠C = 90, m∠A = 63, and AB = 10. If BC is represented by a, then which equation can be used to find a?

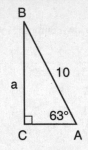

(1) $\sin 63° = \frac{a}{10}$
(3) $\tan 63° = \frac{a}{10}$
(2) $a = 10 \cos 63°$
(4) $a = \tan 27°$

23 If point R′(6,3) is the image of point R(2,1) under a dilation with respect to the origin, what is the constant of the dilation?
(1) 1
(2) 2
(3) 3
(4) 6

24 What is an equation of a line that passes through the point (0,3) and is perpendicular to the line whose equation is y = 2x − 1?
(1) $y = -2x + 3$
(3) $y = -\frac{1}{2}x + 3$
(2) $y = 2x + 3$
(4) $y = \frac{1}{2}x + 3$

25 What is an equation of the function shown in the accompanying diagram?

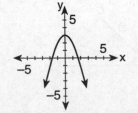

(1) $y = x^2 + 3$
(3) $y = -x^2 - 3$
(2) $y = -x^2 + 3$
(4) $y = (x - 3)^2$

26 What is an equation of the line that is parallel to the y-axis and passes through the point (2,4)?

(1) $x = 2$ (3) $x = 4$
(2) $y = 2$ (4) $y = 4$

27 In the accompanying diagram, the altitude to the hypotenuse of right triangle ABC is 8.

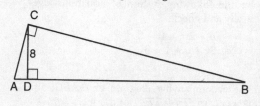

The altitude divides the hypotenuse into segments whose measures may be

(1) 8 and 12   (3) 6 and 10
(2) 3 and 24   (4) 2 and 32

28 If the coordinates of the center of a circle are (−3,1) and the radius is 4, what is an equation of the circle?

(1) $(x - 3)^2 + (y + 1)^0 = 4$
(2) $(x + 3)^2 + (y - 1)^2 = 16$
(3) $(x + 3)^2 + (y - 1)^2 = 4$
(4) $(x - 3)^2 + (y + 1)^2 = 16$

29 Which expression is a solution for the equation $2x^2 - x = 7$?

(1) $\frac{-1 \pm \sqrt{57}}{2}$ (3) $\frac{-1 \pm \sqrt{57}}{4}$

(2) $\frac{1 \pm \sqrt{57}}{2}$ (4) $\frac{1 \pm \sqrt{57}}{4}$

30 If the complement of $\angle A$ is greater than the supplement of $\angle B$, which statement *must* be true?

(1) $m\angle A + m\angle B = 180$
(2) $m\angle A + m\angle B = 90$
(3) $m\angle A < m\angle B$
(4) $m\angle A > m\angle B$

31 How many different four-person committees can be formed from a group of six boys and four girls?

(1) $\frac{10!}{4!}$ (3) $_6C_2 \bullet {_4C_2}$

(2) $_{10}P_4$ (4) $_{10}C_4$

32 Which equation represents the axis of symmetry of the graph of the equation $y = x^2 - 4x - 12$?

(1) $y = 4$ (3) $y = -2$
(2) $x = 2$ (4) $x = -4$

33 What is $\frac{1}{x} + \frac{1}{1 - x}$, $x \neq 1, 0$, expressed as a single fraction?

(1) $\frac{1}{x(1 - x)}$ (3) $\frac{2}{-x}$

(2) $\frac{-1}{x(x + 1)}$ (4) $\frac{1}{x(x - 1)}$

34 In the accompanying diagram, $\overline{RL} \perp \overline{LP}$, $\overline{LR} \perp \overline{RT}$, and M is the midpoint of $\overline{TP}$.

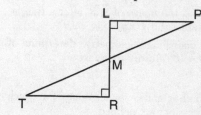

Which method could be used to prove $\triangle TMR \cong \triangle PML$?

(1) SAS ≅ SAS   (3) HL ≅ HL
(2) AAS ≅ AAS   (4) SSS ≅ SSS

Directions (35): Leave all construction lines on the answer sheet.

35 *On the answer sheet*, construct an equilateral triangle in which $\overline{AB}$ is one of the sides.

Answers to the following questions are to be written on paper provided by the school.

Part II

Answer three questions from this part. Clearly indicate the necessary steps, including appropriate formula substitutions, diagrams, graphs, charts, etc. Calculations that may be obtained by mental arithmetic or the calculator do not need to be shown.   [30]

36 a On graph paper, draw the graph of the equation $y = x^2 - 8x + 2$, including all values of x in the interval $0 \leq x \leq 8$.   [6]

   b Find the roots of the equation $x^2 - 8x + 2 = 0$ to the *nearest hundredth*. [*Only an algebraic solution will be accepted.*]   [4]

37 The coordinates of the endpoints of $\overline{AB}$ are $A(-2,4)$ and $B(4,1)$.

   a On a set of axes, graph $\overline{AB}$.   [1]

   b On the same set of axes, graph and state the coordinates of

   (1) $\overline{A'B'}$, the image of $\overline{AB}$ after a reflection in the x-axis   [2]

   (2) $\overline{A''B''}$, the image of $\overline{A'B'}$ after a translation that shifts (x,y) to $(x + 2, y)$ [2]

   c Using coordinate geometry, determine if $\overline{A'B'} \cong \overline{A''B''}$. Justify your answer.   [5]

38 Answer both *a* and *b* for all values for which these expressions are defined.

   a Solve for x: $-\dfrac{2}{5} + \dfrac{x + 4}{x} = 1$ [4]

   b Express the difference in simplest form:

   $$\dfrac{3y}{y^2 - 4} - \dfrac{2}{y + 2}$$ [6]

39 Solve the following system of equations algebraically and check:

$$y = 2x^2 - 4x - 5$$
$$2x + y + 1 = 0$$ [8,2]

40 In the accompanying diagram of $\triangle ABC$, altitude $AD = 13$, $\overline{AB} \cong \overline{AC}$, and m$\angle BAC = 70$.

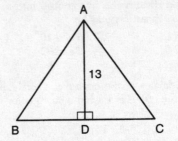

   a Find BC to the *nearest tenth*.   [4]

   b Using the answer from part *a*, find, to the *nearest tenth*, the

   (1) area of $\triangle ABC$ [2]

   (2) perimeter of $\triangle ABC$ [4]

GO RIGHT ON TO THE NEXT PAGE. ⟹

Answers to the following questions are to be written on paper provided by the school.

Part III

Answer one question from this part. Clearly indicate the necessary steps, including appropriate formula substitutions, diagrams, graphs, charts, etc. Calculations that may be obtained by mental arithmetic or the calculator do not need to be shown.   [10]

41 Given: If Sue goes out on Friday night and not on Saturday night, then she does not study.
    If Sue does not fail mathematics, then she studies.
    Sue does not fail mathematics.
    If Sue does not go out on Friday night, then she watches a movie.
    Sue does not watch a movie.

Let A represent: "Sue fails mathematics."
Let B represent: "Sue studies."
Let C represent: "Sue watches a movie."
Let D represent: "Sue goes out on Friday night."
Let E represent: "Sue goes out on Saturday night."

Prove: Sue goes out on Saturday night.   [10]

42 Given: parallelogram $ABCD$, $\overline{DFC}$, $\overline{AEB}$, $\overline{ED}$ bisects $\angle ADC$, and $\overline{FB}$ bisects $\angle ABC$.

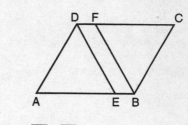

Prove: $\overline{EB} \cong \overline{DF}$ [10]

151

Practice Test 4

Answers

1. The correct answer is 2.

   $1 \star 5 = 1; 2 \star 7 = 1$

   $(1 \star 5) \star (2 \star 7) = 1 \star 1 = 2$

2. The correct answer is 45.

   $2x + 90 = 180$, using vertical angles

   $2x = 90$

   $x = 45$

3. The correct answer is 13.

   $12 \heartsuit 5 =$

   $\sqrt{12^2 + 5^2} = \sqrt{144 + 25} = \sqrt{169} = 13$

4. The correct answer is 8.

   $\dfrac{AB}{AC} = \dfrac{AE}{AD}$ so

   $\dfrac{6}{9} = \dfrac{AE}{AE + 4}$ Cross multiply.

   $6AE + 24 = 9AE$

   $24 = 3AE$ Divide both sides by 3.

   $8 = AE$

5. The correct answer is 60.

   $\dfrac{5!}{2!} = \dfrac{5 \cdot 4 \cdot 3 \cdot \cancel{2 \cdot 1}}{\cancel{2 \cdot 1}} = 60$

   5! because 5 letters, 2! because there are 2 N's.

6. The correct answer is 504.

   $\dfrac{9!}{3!5!} = \dfrac{9 \cdot 8 \cdot 7 \cdot \cancel{6} \cdot \cancel{5!}}{\cancel{3 \cdot 2 \cdot 1} \cdot \cancel{5!}} = 504$

7. The correct answer is 125.

   $m\angle CAB + m\angle C = m\angle CBD$

   $m\angle CAB + 75 = 130$

   $m\angle CAB = 55$

   $m\angle CAB + m\angle CAE = 180$

   $55 + m\angle CAE = 180$

   $m\angle CAE = 125$

8. The correct answer is $\dfrac{1}{2}$.

   Since the sum of the angles of a triangle is $180°$, $m\angle A = 30$. The ratio is $\dfrac{30}{60} = \dfrac{1}{2}$.

9. The correct answer is $\overline{AC}$.

   $m\angle A + m\angle B + m\angle C = 180$

   $3x + 40 + 8x + 35 + 10x = 180$

   $21x + 75 = 180$

   $21x = 105$

   $x = 5$

   $m\angle A = 3(5) + 40 = 55$

   $m\angle B = 8(5) + 35 = 75$

   $m\angle C = 10(5) = 50$

   $\angle B$ is largest angle, so $\overline{AC}$ is the longest side.

10. The correct answer is $\frac{1}{15}$.

    10 total books, choosing two. There are

    $_{10}C_2$ ways. $_{10}C_2 = \frac{10!}{8!2!} = 45$. The number of

    ways of choosing 2 science books out of 3 is

    $_3C_2 = \frac{3!}{2!1!} = 3$.

    The probability is $\frac{3}{45} = \frac{1}{15}$.

11. The correct answer is $\frac{2}{3}$.

    Factor then cancel common factors.

    $\frac{\cancel{(x-3)}\cancel{(x+2)}}{3\cancel{(x-3)}} \cdot \frac{2}{\cancel{x+2}} = \frac{2}{3}$

12. The correct answer is 50.

    let $m\angle B = x$, then $m\angle A = 2x + 30$

    $m\angle A + m\angle B = 180;\quad 2x + 30 + x = 180$

    $3x + 30 = 180$

    $3x = 150$

    $x = 50$

13. The correct answer is $(2, 0)$.

    midpoint:

    $\left(\frac{-6 + 10}{2}, \frac{2 + (-2)}{2}\right) = \left(\frac{4}{2}, \frac{0}{2}\right) = (2,0)$

14. The correct answer is 14.

    The base has endpoints $(1, 2)$ and $(8, 2)$, so

    the base has a length of $8 - 1 = 7$.

    The height has endpoints $(1, 2)$ to $(1, 6)$ a

    length of $6 - 2 = 4$.

    Area $= \frac{1}{2}(7)(4) = 14$

15. The correct answer is 5.

    $\sqrt{[-2 - (-1)]^2 + [-5 - (-1)]^2}$

    $= \sqrt{3^2 + (-4)^2}$

    $= \sqrt{9 + 16} = \sqrt{25} = 5$

16. The correct answer is 80.

    $m\angle BAC + m\angle ABC + m\angle C = 180.$

    $\frac{1}{2} m\angle BAC + \frac{1}{2} m\angle ABC + m\angle D = 180;$

    $\frac{1}{2} m\angle BAC + \frac{1}{2} m\angle ABC + 130 = 180;$

    $\frac{1}{2} m\angle BAC + \frac{1}{2} m\angle ABC = 50;$

    $\frac{1}{2} (m\angle BAC + m\angle ABC) = 50;$ so

    $m\angle BAC + m\angle ABC = 100.$
    Thus $m\angle C = 80.$

17. The correct answer is 4.

    The set of points 5 cm from P forms a circle. The set of points 3 cm from line m would be 2 lines, one above m, one below. The two lines intersect the circle in 4 places.

18. The correct answer is 6.4.

    The diagonals bisect each other forming a right triangle where the hypotenuse is the side of the rhombus,

    $4^2 + 5^2 = s^2$

    $16 + 25 = s^2, 41 = s^2, s = \sqrt{41} = 6.4$

19. The correct answer is (4).

    Draw a figure to see things more clearly.

    Look at choice (1). Angle ADB is an exterior angle of triangle BCD. So $m\angle ADB = m\angle C + m\angle DBC$. So $m\angle ADB > m\angle C$. Now $m\angle C = m\angle A$, because angles C and A are opposite the equal sides AB and BC. So $m\angle ADB > m\angle A$. Discard choice (1). Now consider choice (2). Angle CDB is an exterior angle of triangle ABD. So $m\angle CDB > m\angle A$. Now $m\angle C = m\angle A$, so $m\angle CDB > m\angle C$, so $m\angle CDB > m\angle C$. Discard choice (2). Now consider choice (3). In triangle ABD, we now know that $m\angle ADB > m\angle A$. So $AB > BD$ because in a triangle a side opposite a greater angle is greater than a side opposite a smaller angle. Discard choice (3). Since all 3 incorrect choice have been discarded, we know that choice 4 must be correct. Also, we have actually proved that choice (4), $AB > BD$, must be correct.

20. The correct answer is (1).

    From m and $m\rightarrow p$ we have p by the law of detachment. From $r\rightarrow\sim p$ we have $p\rightarrow\sim r$ by the law of contrapositive. From p and $p\rightarrow\sim r$ we have $\sim r$ by the law of detachment.

21. The correct answer is (3).

    It will change the sign of the x-value.

22. The correct answer is (1).

    Because $\sin 63° = \dfrac{\text{opp}}{\text{hyp}} = \dfrac{a}{10}$

23. The correct answer is (3).

    Because both values have been tripled.

24. The correct answer is (3).

    The slope of $y = 2x - 1$ is 2, since the equation is solved for y and 2 is the coefficient of x. The slope of a perpendicular line will be $-\dfrac{1}{2}$.
    The equation of the line is
    $y = mx + b$.
    $m = -\dfrac{1}{2}$ and $b = 3$.

25. The correct answer is (2).

    The coefficient of x^2 will be negative because the graph is pointing down. The value on the graph when $x = 0$ is $y = 3$.

26. The correct answer is (1).

    Lines parallel to the y-axis have the form $x = $ number and the x-value is 2.

27. The correct answer is 4.

    We need $\dfrac{AD}{CD} = \dfrac{CD}{BD}$ Since $\triangle ADC$ is
    similar to $\triangle CDB$

    So $\dfrac{AD}{8} = \dfrac{8}{BD}$ Cross multiply

    $AD \times BD = 64$

28. The correct answer is (2).

    The equation of a circle is $(x - h)^2 + (y - k)^2 = r^2$ where (h, k) is center and r is radius.
    $[x - (-3)]^2 + (y - 1)^2 = 4^2$
    $(x + 3)^2 + (y - 1)^2 = 16$

29. The correct answer is (4).

    $2x^2 - x = 7$
    $2x^2 - x - 7 = 0$
    $x = \dfrac{1 \pm \sqrt{(-1)^2 - 4(2)(-7)}}{2(2)} = \dfrac{1 \pm \sqrt{1 + 56}}{4}$
    $= \dfrac{1 \pm \sqrt{57}}{4}$

30. The correct answer is (3).

    Complement of $\angle A$ is $90 - m\angle A$

    Supplement of $\angle B$ is $180 - m\angle B$

    $90 - m\angle A > 180 - m\angle B$

    $-m\angle A > 90 - m\angle B$ Multiply by -1.

    $m\angle A < -90 + m\angle B$

    $m\angle A < m\angle B - 90$

    $m\angle A < m\angle B - 90$

31. The correct answer is (4).

    10 total people, choosing 4 =

    $_{10}C_4$

32. The correct answer is (2).

    $y = ax^2 - bx + c$

    Here, $a = 1$, $b = -4$ and $c = 12$. The

    equation of the axis of symmetry is x

    $= -\dfrac{b}{2a} = \dfrac{-4}{2(1)} = \dfrac{4}{2} = 2$. Thus $x = 2$.

33. The correct answer is (1).

    Common denominator is $x(1 - x)$

    $$\dfrac{(1 - x)}{x(1 - x)} + \dfrac{x}{x(1 - x)} = \dfrac{1 - x}{x(1 - x)} + \dfrac{x}{x(1 - x)}$$

    $$= \dfrac{1}{x(1 - x)}$$

34. The correct answer is (2).

    $\overline{LM} \cong \overline{MR}$, $\angle TMR$ and $\angle LMP$ are vertical angles so they are equal, and $\angle MRT \cong \angle MLP$ because they are both right angles, so the triangles are congruent by AAS.

35.

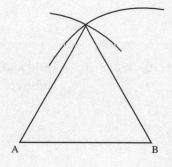

1. Swing arcs from A and B that are the length of $\overline{AB}$

2. Intersection of arcs is 3rd point of triangle.

36. a.

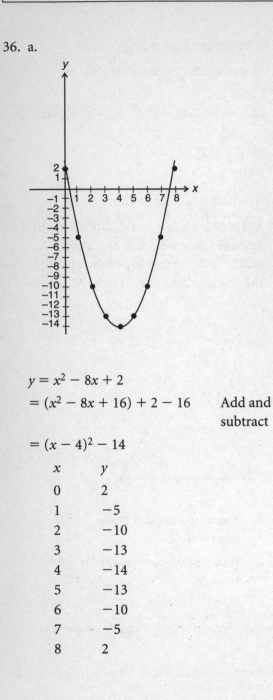

$y = x^2 - 8x + 2$

$= (x^2 - 8x + 16) + 2 - 16$ Add and subtract

$= (x - 4)^2 - 14$

x	y
0	2
1	−5
2	−10
3	−13
4	−14
5	−13
6	−10
7	−5
8	2

b. 7.74 and 0.26

$x^2 - 8x + 2 = 0$

$x = \dfrac{8 \pm \sqrt{8^2 - 4(1)(2)}}{2(1)} = \dfrac{8 \pm \sqrt{64 - 8}}{2} =$

$\dfrac{8 \pm \sqrt{56}}{2}$

$\dfrac{8 + \sqrt{56}}{2} = 7.74 \qquad \dfrac{8 - \sqrt{56}}{2} = 0.26$

37. a.

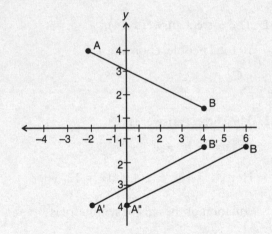

b. (1) $A' = (-2, -4)$ $B' = (4, -1)$
(see graph)
(2) $A'' = (-2 + 2, -4) = (0, -4)$
$B'' = (4 + 2, -1) = (6, -1)$
(see graph)

c. $A'B' =$

$\sqrt{[4-1(2)]^2 + [-1-(-4)]^2} = \sqrt{6^2+3^2}$

$\sqrt{36+9} = \sqrt{45}$

$A''B'' =$

$\sqrt{(6-0)^2 + [-1-(-4)]^2} = \sqrt{6^2+3^2}$

$\sqrt{36+9} = \sqrt{45}$

Since the lengths are equal, the segments are congruent.

38. a. $x = 10$

$-\dfrac{2}{5} + \dfrac{x+4}{x} = 1$ Multiply by LCD of $5x$.

$-2x + 5(x+4) = 5x$

$-2x + 5x + 20 = 5x$

$3x + 20 = 5x$

$20 = 2x$

$10 = x$

b. $\dfrac{y+4}{(y+2)(y-2)}$

$y^2 - 4 = (y+2)(y-2)$

so LCD is $(y-2)(y+2)$

$\dfrac{3y}{(y+2)(y-2)} - \dfrac{2(y-2)}{(y+2)(y-2)} =$

$\dfrac{3y}{(y+2)(y-2)} - \dfrac{2y-4}{(y+2)(y-2)} =$

$\dfrac{3y-(2y-4)}{(y+2)(y-2)} = \dfrac{3y-2y+4}{(y+2)(y-2)} =$

$\dfrac{y+4}{(y+2)(y-2)}$

39. The correct answer is $(2, -5)$ and $(-1,1)$.

Solve $3x + y + 1 = 0$ for y, yielding $y = -1 - 2x$

Substitute into $y = 2x^2 - 4x - 5$ yielding

$-1 - 2x = 2x^2 - 4x - 5$

$0 = 2x^2 - 2x - 4$

$0 = 2(x^2 - x - 2)$

$0 = 2(x-2)(x+1)$

$x - 2 = 0 \qquad x + 1 = 0$

$x = 2 \qquad\qquad x = -1$

$x = 2$

$y = -1 - 2(2) = -1 - 4 = -5$

$x = -1$

$y = -1 - 2(-1) = -1 + 2 = 1$

Check

$-5 = 2(2^2) - 4(2) - 5$

$-5 = 2(4) - 8 - 5$

$-5 = -8 - 8 - 5$

$-5 = -5$

$2(2) + -5 + 1 = 0$

$4 - 5 + 1 = 0$

$0 = 0$

$(2, -5)$ is a solution.

$1 = 2(-1)^2 - 4(-1) - 5$

$1 = 2(1) + 4 - 5$

$1 = 1$

$2(-1) + 1 + 1 = 0$

$-2 + 1 + 1 = 0$

$0 = 0$

$(-1, 1)$ is a solution.

40. a. The correct answer is 18.2.

Since m$\angle BAC = 70$, m$\angle B$ + m$\angle C =$ 110 and m$\angle B$ = m$\angle C$ = 55.

$$\tan 55° = \frac{\text{opp}}{\text{adj}} = \frac{13}{BD}$$

$BD \tan 55° = 13$

$$BD = \frac{13}{\tan 55} = 9.1 \quad BC = 2BD = 18.2$$

b.(1) 118.3

$$\text{Area} = \frac{1}{2}(BC)(AD)$$

$$= \frac{1}{2}(18.2)(13) = 118.3$$

(2) 49.9

$$\sin 55° = \frac{\text{opp}}{\text{hyp}} = \frac{13}{AB}$$

$AB \sin 55° = 13$

$$AB = \frac{13}{\sin 55°} = 15.87 = AC$$

Perimeter = 15.87 + 18.2 + 15.87 = 49.94

41. | *Steps of direct proof* | *Reasons* |
|---|---|
| 1. $D \wedge \sim E \rightarrow \sim B$ | Given |
| 2. $\sim A \rightarrow B$ | Given |
| 3. $\sim A$ | Given |
| 4. $\sim D \rightarrow C$ | Given |
| 5. $\sim C$ | Given |
| 6. B | Law of detachment applied to steps 2 and 3 |
| 7. $B \rightarrow \sim (D \sim E)$ | Law of contrapositive applied to step 1 |
| 8. $\sim (D \sim E)$ | Law of detachment applied to steps 6 and 7 |
| 9. $\sim D \sim E$ | De Morgan's law applied to step 8 |
| 10. $\sim C \rightarrow D$ | Law of contrapositive applied to step 4 |
| 11. D | Law of detachment applied to steps 5 and 10 |
| 12. $\sim E$ | Law of disjunctive inference applied to steps 9 and 11 |

42. Since $ABCD$ is a parallelogram, $\angle A \cong \angle C$ and $\angle D \cong \angle B$, $\overline{AD} \cong \overline{CB}$

    Since $\angle D \cong \angle B$ then $m\angle D = m\angle B$ and $\frac{1}{2} m\angle D = \frac{1}{2} m\angle B$

    $m\angle ADE = \frac{1}{2} m\angle D$ and $m\angle FBC = \frac{1}{2} m\angle B$. Thus,

    $m\angle ADE = m\angle FBC$ and $\angle ADE \cong \angle FBC$.

    Then $\triangle ADE \cong \triangle CBF$ by ASA. So $\overline{AE} \cong \overline{FC}$ because these are corresponding parts of the congruent triangles. Also $\overline{AB} \cong \overline{DC}$ because opposite sides of a parallelogram are equal. So $AB = DC$

    $\qquad AE = FC$

    Therefore $AB - AE = DC - FC$.

    So $EB = DF$

    So $\overline{EB} \cong \overline{DF}$

Practice Test 5

Answer 30 questions from this part. Each correct answer will receive 2 credits. No partial credit will be allowed. Write your answers in the spaces provided on the separate answer sheet. Where applicable, answers may be left in radical form. [60]

1 In rectangle $ABCD$, $AC = 2x + 15$ and $BD = 4x - 5$. Find x.

2 If the measures of three angles of a quadrilateral are 30, 70, and 110, find the measure of the fourth angle.

3 The perimeter of $\triangle ABC$ is 30. Find the perimeter of the triangle formed by joining the midpoints of the sides of $\triangle ABC$.

4 If $p \# q$ is defined as $3p \div 2q$, find the value of $4 \# 1$.

5 In $\triangle LMN$, P is a point on $\overline{LM}$ and Q is a point on $\overline{LN}$ such that $\overline{PQ} \parallel \overline{MN}$. If $LP = 4$, $PM = 3$, and $QN = 9$, what is the length of $\overline{LQ}$?

6 Evaluate: $_{20}C_{19}$

7 In $\triangle ABC$, the measure of $\angle A$ is 50 and the measure of an exterior angle at vertex B is 125. Which is the longest side of the triangle?

8 If 2 is a root of the equation $x^2 + kx + 6 = 0$, find the value of k.

9 The ratio of the corresponding sides of two similar triangles is 7:5. Find the ratio of their perimeters.

10 In the accompanying diagram, $\triangle ABC$ is a right triangle and $\overline{CD}$ is the altitude to hypotenuse $\overline{AB}$. If $AD = 4$ and $DB = 16$, find the length of $\overline{CD}$.

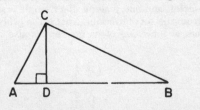

11 Find, in radical form, the length of the line segment joining points (1,5) and (3,9).

12 In parallelogram $ABCD$, m$\angle A$ is 30 more than m$\angle B$. Find the measure of $\angle D$.

13 Find the roots of the equation $x^2 + 8x + 15 = 0$.

14 Find the slope of the line that passes through points $L(4,5)$ and $N(3,-4)$.

15 How many different arrangements of 7 letters can be formed from the letters in the name "SOLOMON"?

16 In parallelogram $ABCD$, the coordinates of A are (7,3) and of C are (5,-1). What are the coordinates of the intersection of the diagonals?

17 Find the length of a diagonal of a square whose perimeter is 20.

18 If the equation of a circle is $x^2 + y^2 = 34$, what is the length of the radius?

Directions (19–34): For *each* question chosen, write on the separate answer sheet the *numeral* preceding the word or expression that best completes the statement or answers the question.

19 In the system $(S,*)$ defined below, what is the solution to the equation $x * x = x$?

*	a	b	c	d
a	c	d	a	b
b	d	a	b	c
c	a	b	c	d
d	b	c	d	a

(1) a (3) c
(2) b (4) d

20 The table below defines the operation ⊕ for the set of elements $\{w,x,y,z\}$. What is the identity element?

⊕	w	x	y	z
w	x	z	w	y
x	z	y	x	w
y	w	x	y	z
z	y	w	z	x

(1) w (3) y
(2) x (4) z

21 Which equation describes a set of points equidistant from the x-axis and the y-axis?

(1) $x = y$ (3) $y = 3$
(2) $x + y = 1$ (4) $x = -7$

22 Which set of numbers can *not* represent the measures of the angles of a triangle?

(1) $\{35,125,10\}$ (3) $\{30,110,40\}$
(2) $\{20,100,60\}$ (4) $\{97,59,24\}$

23 If the points $(3,5)$, $(4,2)$, and $(5,k)$ lie on a straight line, the value of k is

(1) 1   (3) -1
(2) 0   (4) -2

24 Which statement is logically equivalent to $\sim(\sim a \lor b)$?

(1) $a \lor \sim b$ (3) $\sim a \lor \sim b$
(2) $a \land \sim b$ (4) $\sim a \land \sim b$

25 The coordinates of the turning point of the parabola whose equation is $y = x^2 - 6x + 8$ are

(1) $(3,35)$ (3) $(-3,35)$
(2) $(-3,-1)$ (4) $(3,-1)$

26 If the lengths of two sides of a triangle are 7 and 10, the length of the third side may be

(1) 1   (3) 3
(2) 2   (4) 4

27 Given the true statements:

$$p \to r$$
$$q \to \sim r$$
$$p$$

Which conclusion is valid?

(1) q (3) $\sim r$
(2) $\sim q$ (4) $\sim p$

28 Which is the negation of the statement "All squares are rectangles"?

(1) Some squares are not rectangles.
(2) Some squares are rectangles.
(3) All squares are not rectangles.
(4) No squares are rectangles.

29 Which pair of points will determine a line parallel to the y-axis?

(1) $(2,3)$ and $(-1,3)$ (3) $(3,2)$ and $(3,-1)$
(2) $(2,2)$ and $(-3,-3)$ (4) $(2,-2)$ and $(-2,2)$

30 Which is an example of a quadrilateral whose diagonals are congruent but do *not* bisect each other?

(1) a square
(2) an isosceles trapezoid
(3) a rhombus
(4) a rectangle

31 The elements a, b, c, and d form commutative group R with respect to @. Which expression is equivalent to $a \, @ \, c$ in group R?

(1) b (3) $a \, @ \, a^{-1}$
(2) $c \, @ \, a$ (4) $(a^{-1} \, @ \, c^{-1})$

32 A set contains three triangles: one equilateral, one isosceles, and one scalene. If a triangle is selected from the set at random, what is the probability that at least one of its medians is also an altitude?

(1) 1   (3) $\frac{1}{3}$
(2) 0   (4) $\frac{2}{3}$

33 Which is an equation of the line that has a *y*-intercept of –2 and is parallel to the line whose equation is $4y = 3x + 7$?

(1) $y = \frac{3}{4}x - 2$ (3) $y = \frac{4}{3}x - 2$

(2) $y = \frac{3}{4}x + 2$ (4) $y = -\frac{4}{3}x - 2$

34 How many points are 2 centimeters from a given line and 2 centimeters from a given point on that line?

(1) 1   (3) 3
(2) 2   (4) 0

Directions (35): Leave all construction lines on the answer sheet.

35 *On the answer sheet*, construct the median to side $\overline{AC}$ in $\triangle ABC$.

Answers to the following questions are to be written on paper provided by the school.

Part II

Answer three questions from this part. Show all work unless otherwise directed. [30]

36 At random, Coach Smith chooses her 5-member math team from a club that consists of 3 boys and 5 girls.

a How many different 5-member teams can be chosen? [2]

b What is the probability that the team has only 1 boy? [2]

c What is the probability that the team has only 1 girl? [2]

d What is the probability that Susan, a member of the club, is *not* chosen for the team? [4]

37 The equation of line $\overleftrightarrow{AB}$ is $x = 2$.

a Describe fully the locus of points d units from line $\overleftrightarrow{AB}$. [2]

b Describe fully the locus of points 1 unit from the origin. [2]

c How many points satisfy the conditions in parts a and b simultaneously for the following values of d?

(1) $d = 2$ [2]
(2) $d = 3$ [2]
(3) $d = 4$ [2]

38 a Find the roots of the equation $x^2 - 2x - 4 = 0$. [Answer may be left in radical form.] [3]

b On graph paper, draw the graph of the equation $y = x^2 - 2x - 4$ using all integral values of x such that $-2 \le x \le 4$. [5]

c Based on the graph drawn in part b, between which two positive consecutive integers does the value of $y = 0$ lie? [2]

39 Find the area of quadrilateral $ABCD$ with vertices $A(5,2)$, $B(0,5)$, $C(-2,-2)$, and $D(0,0)$. [10]

40 Jean, Bill, and Mel are competing in a game of marbles. At the start of the game, each has the same number of marbles. After Jean wins two marbles from Bill and two marbles from Mel, the number that Jean has is the product of the numbers remaining for Bill and Mel. How many marbles did each have at the start of the game? [*Only an algebraic solution will be accepted.*] [5,5]

Answers to the following questions are to be written on paper provided by the school.

Part III

Answer one question from this part. Show all work unless otherwise directed. [10]

41 Given: If Cathy gets married and moves to Germany, her mother will be lonely.
Cathy gets married.
Her mother is not lonely.

Let C represent: "Cathy gets married."
Let G represent: "Cathy moves to Germany."
Let L represent: "Her mother is lonely."

Prove: Cathy does not move to Germany. [10]

42 The vertices of $\triangle ABC$ are $A(-2,3)$, $B(0,-3)$, and $C(4,1)$. Prove, by means of coordinate geometry, that

a $\triangle ABC$ is isosceles [4]

b the median to side $\overline{BC}$ is also the altitude to side $\overline{BC}$ [6]

Practice Test 5

Answers

1. The correct answer is 10.

   Diagonals are equal.

   $2x + 15 = 4x - 5$

   $20 = 2x$

   $10 = x$

2. The correct answer is 150.

   The sum should be 360.

   $30 + 70 + 110 + x = 360$

   $210 + x = 360$

   $x = 150$

3. The correct answer is 15.

   If a line segment connects the midpoints of a triangle, it is parallel to the third side and has a length half of the length of the third side. So the perimeter of this triangle is $\frac{1}{2}(30) = 15$.

4. The correct answer is 6.

   $4 \# 1 = 3(4) \div 2(1) = 12 \div 2 = 6$

5. The correct answer is 12.

   $\frac{LQ}{LP} = \frac{QN}{PM}$ $\frac{x}{4} = \frac{9}{3}$ Cross multiply.

   $3x = 36$

   $x = 12$

6. The correct answer is 20.

   $_{20}C_{19} = \frac{20!}{1!19!} = \frac{20 \cdot 19!}{1!19!} = 20$

7. $\overline{AB}$

   The interior angle at B is 55, m∠A = 50 so m∠C = 75. Since C is the largest angle, the side opposite angle C, which is AB, is the longest.

8. The correct answer is −5.

   Plug in 2, $(2)^2 + k(2) + 6 = 0$

   $4 + 2k + 6 = 0$

   $2k + 10 = 0$

   $2k = -10$

   $k = -5$

9. 7:5

   The ratio remains the same.

10. The correct answer is 8.

    $\triangle ADC$ is similar to $\triangle CDB$ so

    $\frac{AD}{CD} = \frac{CD}{DB}$

    $\frac{4}{CD} = \frac{CD}{16}$ Cross multiply.

    $64 = (CD)^2$ so $8 = CD$

11. $2\sqrt{5}$

$$\begin{aligned}
d &= \sqrt{(3-1)^2 + (9-5)^2} \\
&= \sqrt{2^2 + 4^2} \\
&= \sqrt{4 + 16} \\
&= \sqrt{4 \cdot 5} \\
&= \sqrt{4} \cdot \sqrt{5} \\
&= 2\sqrt{5}
\end{aligned}$$

12. The correct answer is 75.

$\angle A$ and $\angle B$ are supplementary. If $x =$ m$\angle B$ then $x + 30 =$ m$\angle A$ and $x + x + 30 = 180$; $2x = 150$, $x = 75$. $\angle B$ and $\angle D$ have the same measure, so m$\angle D = 75$.

13. $-5, -3$

$$x^2 + 8x + 15 = 0$$
$$(x + 5)(x + 3) = 0$$
$$x + 5 = 0 \quad x + 3 = 0$$
$$x = -5 \quad x = -3$$

14. The correct answer is 9.

slope $= \dfrac{-4 - 5}{3 - 4} = \dfrac{-9}{-1} = 9$

15. 840

There are 7! ways to arrange 7 letters, but there are 3! ways to arrange the 3 Os so 7! must be divided by 3!.

$\dfrac{7!}{3!} = \dfrac{7 \cdot 6 \cdot 5 \cdot 4 \cdot 3!}{3!} = 840$

16. $(6, 1)$

$\overline{AC}$ is a diagonal and the diagonals will intersect at the midpoint.

$\left(\dfrac{7 + 5}{2}, \dfrac{3 - 1}{2}\right) = (6,1)$

17. $5\sqrt{2}$

If the perimeter is 20 each side is 5. Use the Pythagorean Theorem, $5^2 + 5^2 = d^2$; $25 + 25 = d^2$; $50 = d^2$

$d = \sqrt{50} = 5\sqrt{2}$

18. $\sqrt{34}$

The radius is $\sqrt{34}$.

19. The correct answer is (3).

Check all possibilities $a * a = c$, $b * b = a$, $c * c = c$, and $d * d = a$.

20. The correct answer is (3).

Determine what element $\oplus$ anything yields the same thing.

21. The correct answer is (1).

$y = x$ bisects quadrants I and III.

22. The correct answer is (1).

The sum must be 180 in a triangle.

23. The correct answer is (3).

    Slope of $(3, 5)$ to $(4, 2)$ is

    $$\frac{2-5}{4-3} = \frac{-3}{1} = -3$$

    slope of $(3, 5)$ to $(5, k)$ is

    $$\frac{k-5}{5-3} = \frac{k-5}{2}$$

    Need $\dfrac{k-5}{-2} = -3$ so

    $k - 5 = 6$; $k = -6 + 1$, $k = -1$

24. The correct answer is (2).

    $\sim (\sim a \vee b) = \sim (\sim a) \wedge \sim b = a \wedge \sim b$

25. The correct answer is (4).

    The x-coordinate of the turning point of the parabola whose equation is $y = ax^2 + bx + c$ is $-\dfrac{b}{2a}$. Here, the equation of the parabola is $y = x^2 - 6x + 8$, so $a = 1$, $b = -6$, and $c = 8$. The x-coordinate of the turning point is $-\dfrac{b}{2a} = -\dfrac{-6}{2(1)}$ $= 3$. The y-coordinate is $3^2 - 6(3) + 8 = 9 - 18 + 8 = -1$.

    The turning point is $(3, -1)$.

26. The correct answer is (4).

    The sum of the two smallest sides must be larger than the largest side.

27. The correct answer is (2).

    From $p \rightarrow r$ and p, we have r by the law of detachment. From $q \rightarrow \sim r$, we have $r \rightarrow \sim q$ by the law of contrapositive. From r and $r \rightarrow \sim q$ and. We have $\sim q$ by the law of detachment.

28. The correct answer is (1).

    Negation of all are is some are not.

29. The correct answer is (3).

    Lines parallel to y-axis are $x =$ number so the x-values must be the same.

30. The correct answer is (2).

    This is the only figure whose diagonals do not bisect each other.

31. The correct answer is (2).

    Commutative means the order can be changed without changing the result.

32. The correct answer is (4).

    In both an equilateral and isosceles triangle at least one median is also an altitude.

33. The correct answer is (1).

    Solve $4y = 3x + 7$ for y; $y = \frac{3}{4}x + \frac{7}{4}$.

    $\frac{3}{4}$ is the slope, $\frac{7}{4}$ the y-intercept.

    To be parallel you need a slope of $\frac{3}{4}$

    $y = \frac{3}{4}x + $ intercept, so $y = \frac{3}{4}x - 2$.

34. The correct answer is (2).

    Two centimeters from a point yields a circle and 2 points are also 2 cm from the line.

35.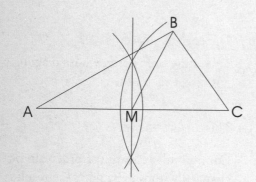

    Find the midpoint of $\overline{AC}$ by swinging two arcs. Mark midpoint M. Median is $\overline{BM}$.

36. a. 56

    $_8C_5 = \dfrac{8 \cdot 7 \cdot 6 \cdot 5}{3 \cdot 2 \cdot 1 \cdot 5!} = 56$

b. $\dfrac{15}{56}$

There are $_3C_1 = 3$ ways to choose 1 boy.

There are $_5C_4 = 5$ ways to choose 4 girls.

Thus, $3 \cdot 5 = 15$ ways to choose 1 boy and 4 girls. Probability is $\dfrac{15}{56}$.

c. 0

There are 5 members of the team, if only 1 is a girl then 4 are boys. Since there are only 3 boys this is not possible.

d. $\dfrac{3}{8}$

If Susan is not chosen, there are 7 people to choose from, so there are $_7C_5 = 21$ ways.

Probability $\dfrac{21}{56}$ or $\dfrac{3}{8}$.

37. a. This would be all points d units from $x = 2$. Two lines, each d units away, one to the right and one to the left. One would have the equation $x = 2 + d$ and one would have the equation $x = 2 - d$.

b. This would be a circle centered at $(0, 0)$ with radius 1. The equation is $x^2 + y^2 = 1$.

c. (1) 2

The equations of the lines would be $x = 4$ and $x = 0$. The line $x = 4$ does not intersect the circle, but $x = 0$ intersects the circle at $(0, 1)$ and $(0, -1)$.

(2) 1

The equations would be $x = 5$ and $x = -1$. The line $x = 5$ does not intersect the circle, but $x = -1$ intersects the circle at $(-1, 0)$.

(3) 0

The equations would be $x = 6$ and $x = -2$. Neither line will intersect the circle.

38. a. $1 \pm \sqrt{5}$

$x^2 - 2x - 4 = 0$

$a = 1,\ b = -2,\ \text{and}\ c = -4$

$x = \dfrac{2 \pm \sqrt{(-2)^2 - 4(1)(-1)}}{2(1)}$

$ = \dfrac{2 \pm \sqrt{4 + 16}}{2}$

$ = \dfrac{2 \pm \sqrt{20}}{2}$

$ = \dfrac{2 \pm 2\sqrt{5}}{2}$

$ = 1 \pm \sqrt{5}$

b.

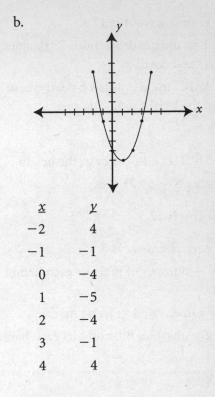

x	y
-2	4
-1	-1
0	-4
1	-5
2	-4
3	-1
4	4

c. 3 and 4

The graph crosses the x-axis on the positive side between 3 and 4.

39. The correct answer is 17.5.

Think of the quadrilateral as 2 triangles, $\triangle BCD$ and $\triangle ABD$.

For $\triangle ABD$ use $\overline{BD}$ as the base, the base is 5 and the height is 5. The area is $\frac{1}{2}(5) = \frac{25}{2} = 12.5$.

For $\triangle BCD$ use $\overline{BD}$ as base, the height is 2. The area is $\frac{1}{2}(5)(2) = 5$.

Total area is $12.5 + 5 = 17.5$.

40. The correct answer is 5.

Let x = number of marbles each had to start.

After game, $x + 4$ = Jean's marbles.

$x - 2$ = marbles Bill and Mel each have.

$x + 4 = (x - 2)(x - 2)$

$x + 4 = x^2 - 4x + 4$

$0 = x^2 - 5x$

$0 = x(x - 5)$

$x = 0 \qquad x - 5 = 0$ so $x = 5$

41.

Steps of direct proof	Reasons
1. $C \wedge G \to L$	Given
2. C	Given
3. L	Given
4. $\sim L \to \sim(C \wedge G)$	Law of contrapositive applied to Step 1
5. $\sim(C \wedge G)$	Law of detachment applied to steps 3 and 4
6. $\sim C \vee \sim G$	De Morgan's law applied to step 5
7. $\sim G$	Law of disjunctive inference applied to steps 2 and 6

42. a.

$$AB = \sqrt{[0 - (-2)]^2 + (-3 - 3)^2}$$
$$= \sqrt{2^2 + (-6)^2}$$
$$= \sqrt{4 + 36}$$
$$= \sqrt{40}$$

$$BC = (4 - 0)^2 + (-3 - 1)^2$$
$$= \sqrt{(-4)^2 + (-4)^2}$$
$$= \sqrt{(16 + 16)}$$
$$= \sqrt{32}$$

$$AC = \sqrt{[4 - (-2)]^2 + (1 - 3)^2}$$
$$= \sqrt{6^2 + (-2)^2}$$
$$= \sqrt{36 + 4}$$
$$= \sqrt{40}$$

Thus, $AB = AC$, so $\overline{AB} \cong \overline{AC}$, and the triangle is isosceles.

b. The median passes through the midpoint. The midpoint is

$$\left(\frac{0+4}{2}, \frac{-3+1}{2}\right) = (2, -1).$$

The median goes from $(-2, 3)$ to $(2, -1)$ and has slope of $\frac{-1-3}{2-(-2)} = \frac{-4}{4} = -1.$

The slope of $\overline{BC}$ is $\frac{1-(-3)}{4-0} = \frac{4}{4} = 1.$

Since the slopes are negative reciprocals, the median is perpendicular to $\overline{BC}$, thus an altitude.

Subject Index

A

AAS (angle-angle-side), 56

Acute angle, 63

Addition

    of algebraic fractions, 49

    of polynomials, 43

Algebra

    algebraic fractions, 46–49

    review of skills, 43–46

Alternate interior angles, 59

Analytic geometry, 77–85

Analytic proof, 85

Angles

    acute angle, 63

    alternate interior angles, 59

    angle measures in triangles, 63–64

    angle relationships theorems, 57

    complementary angles, 59

    corresponding angles, 59

    exterior angles, 59

    interior angles, 59

    obtuse angle, 63

    remote interior angles, 60

    right angle, 63

    supplementary angles, 59

    vertical angles, 59

Antecedent, 33

Area

    application to coordinate geometry, 79–80

    of a parallelogram, 79

    of a rectangle, 79

    of a square, 79

    of a trapezoid, 79

    of a triangle, 79

Associative property, 41

Assumptions, 53

Axiomatic systems, 53–54

B

Biconditional statement, 33

C

Circle, 82

   equation of, 82

Closure property, 41

Combinations, 104–105

Commutative property, 41

Complementary angles, 59

Completing the square, 92

Conclusion, 33

Conditional statement, 33

Congruence, 54–57

   congruence, other postulates, 56–57

Conics, 82–83

Conjunction, 33

Consequent, 33

Constructions and Proofs, 71

Contradiction, 33

Contrapositive, 34–35

   Law of Contrapositive, 35

Converse, 34

Corresponding angles, 59

Counting principle, 102

D

De Morgan's laws, 36

Detachment, Law of, 35

Diagonals of a parallelogram, 64–67

Dilations, 82

Direct Proof, 36–37

Disjunction, 33

Disjunctive Inference, Law of, 35–36

Distributive property, 42

Division

   of fractions with polynomial denominators, 48

   of polynomials by monomials, 44–45

E

Equation

   of a circle, 82

   of a line, 78–79

   of a parabola, 83

Euclidean geometry, 53–71

Event, 101

Experiment, 101

Exterior angles, 59

F

Factoring, 45

Fields, 50

Finite systems, 50

Fractional equations, 91

G

Geometry

    analytic, 77–85

    Euclidean, 53–71

Groups, 49–50

H

HL (hypotenuse-leg), 56

Hypothesis, 33

I

Identity element, 41

Image, 80

Indirect Proof, 37–38

Inequalities, Properties of, 89

Infinite systems, 50

Interior angles, 59

Inverse, 34–35

    inverse element, 41

Isosceles triangle theorems, 55–56

L

Law of Contrapositive, 35

Law of Detachment, 35

Law of Disjunctive Inference, 35–36

Law of Syllogism, 36

Laws of Reasoning, 35–36

Length of a segment, 78

Linear equations, 46, 89–90

Linear inequalities, 89–90

Locus, 84

Logic, 33–38

Logical connectives, 33–34

M

Midpoint of a segment, 78

Multiplication

    of fractions with polynomial
    denominators, 48

    of polynomials, 43

N

Negation, 33

O

Obtuse angle, 63

Operation, 41

Ordered arrangement, 103

Ordered pair, 77

Origin, 77

Outcomes, 101

P

Pairs of equations, 95–96

Parabola, 83

Parallel lines, 59, 77

Parallelism, 59–67

    parallelism, theorems and postulates, 60–67

Parallelogram, 64

Permutation, 103–104

Perpendicular lines, 77

Point-slope form, 78

Polynomial denominators, 47–48

Probability, 101–102

Proof, 53

    analytic proof, 85

    direct proof, 36–37

    indirect proof, 37–38

Properties of real numbers, 41–42

Proportions, 90

Pythagorean Theorem, 69

Q

Quadratic equations, 91–94

Quadratic formula, 93

Quadratic-linear pair, 96

R

Reasoning, Laws of, 35–36

Rectangular coordinate system, review of, 77

Reflection

    in a line, 80

    in a point, 81

Relationships of lengths of sides, 58

Remote interior angles, 60

Rhombus, 64

Right angle, 63

Right triangle trigonometry, 71

S

Segment, 78

Similarity, 67–71

  similar polygons, 67

  similar triangles, 67–69

Simplifying algebraic expressions, 44

Simplifying algebraic fractions, 47

Slope, 77

Slope-intercept form, 78

Solving linear equations, 46

Space, 101

Special right triangles, 70–71

Statement, 33

Subtraction of algebraic fractions, 49

Supplementary angles, 59

Syllogism, Law of, 36

System of equations, graphic solution, 83

T

Tautology, 33

Theorems, 53–54

  angle relationships, 57

  isosceles triangle, 55–56

Pythagorean, 69

quadrilaterals, 64–67

relationships of lengths of sides, 58

Transformations, 80–82

Translations, 81

Transversal, 59

Trapezoid, 64

Trigonometry, 71

Truth value, 33

U

Unordered arrangement, 104–105

V

Vertical angles, 59

X

x-axis, 77

x-coordinate, 77

Y

y-axis, 77

y-coordinate, 77